Arthur Campbell

For my mother
Cora Lee Quinn
and daughter
Candace

Arthur Campbell

PIONEER AND PATRIOT
OF THE
"OLD SOUTHWEST"

Hartwell L. Quinn

McFarland & Company, Inc., Publishers
Jefferson, North Carolina, and London

British Library Cataloguing-in-Publication data are available

Library of Congress Cataloguing-in-Publication Data

Quinn, Hartwell L., 1939–
    Arthur Campbell : Pioneer and patriot of the "old Southwest" / by
Hartwell L. Quinn.
      p. cm.
    Includes bibliographical references and index.
    ISBN 0-89950-509-0 (50# alk. paper : lib. bdg.) ∞
    1. Campbell, Arthur, 1742–1811. 2. Pioneers – Southwest, Old –
Biography. 3. Frontier and pioneer life – Southwest, Old.
4. Southwest, Old – History. I. Title.
F396.C29Q56 1990
976'.02'092 – dc20
[B]   89-43628
                                                        CIP

Manufactured in the United States of America

McFarland & Company, Inc., Publishers
  Box 611, Jefferson, North Carolina 28640

Preface

Arthur Campbell was born in Augusta County, Virginia, in 1743 and died in Middlesboro, Kentucky, in 1811. His life spanned the great historical events of the French and Indian War, the American Revolution, the Constitutional Convention of 1787, and the birth of political parties. Tracing his life affords a close-up view of the founding of the American nation.

Campbell's role in defending Southwest Virginia during many years of Indian warfare, his aid to outposts in Kentucky during the Revolution, campaigns against Loyalists, and his part in organizing the expedition against Major Patrick Ferguson at Kings Mountain, are the most obvious contributions he made to his country. Also important was his influence on the growth of democracy. Campbell was a patriot who took literally the philosophy of the Declaration of Independence. One of the more informed and outspoken leaders on the frontier, who demanded equality with the East, he accelerated the development of democracy which has been so much associated with the Old Southwest.

I wish to thank Professor G. Melvin Herndon, of the University of Georgia, who first turned my attention to Colonel Arthur Campbell. A Virginian himself, Professor Herndon provided me with valuable information concerning Virginia history and sources of information. I will forever be indebted to him for his guidance and encouragement.

Likewise, I wish to express my indebtedness to Professor Ronald L. Swofford of DeKalb College, Decatur, Georgia, for urging me to

v

publish this book. Professor Swofford, a North Carolinian, gave me much needed information about the geography of the beautiful region that comprises the Old Southwest.

To Julie Bridges I express my gratitude, not only because she typed the revised manuscript, but also for her support and the many helpful suggestions she made.

My deep appreciation is also extended to Barbara Hickman for the long hours she spent typing the first draft of this work.

And to my friend, Richard Cantrell, I wish to offer my thanks for encouraging me to write.

To my wife, Dana, who not only tolerated a clutter of books and papers in our home while this work was in progress, but who also read the manuscript and gave me many helpful suggestions, I express my deep appreciation.

My thanks also go to Louise Britton of DeKalb College for drawing the maps.

There are many others who contributed to the writing of this book: the staffs of the University of Georgia Library, the DeKalb College Library and the Virginia State Library in Richmond; and Duke University for permission to print "Letter to a Young Man." Also, to all historians whose books and articles about the Old Southwest not only made the writing of this book possible, but made it a thrilling experience, I express my indebtedness and thanks.

Contents

1 Bearing the Yoke

Like many public figures directly involved in the great events of their time, Arthur Campbell was a complex, paradoxical man, both highly respected and bitterly hated by his contemporaries. David Campbell, a former governor of Virginia, wrote of his uncle Arthur, "he was hasty and excitable..., disposed to be overbearing..., often engaged in violent personal quarrels,"[1] and "had more bitter enemies than any man I ever knew in my life."[2] Others have characterized Campbell as "mercenary, cunning, swindling, and dishonorable,"[3] and "severe, haughty, austere..., little disposed to make companions with anyone."[4] Still others saw a completely different Campbell. "During the memorable struggle for independence," wrote William B. Campbell, "no man ... rendered more efficient service than Arthur Campbell ... both in the field against the enemy or in the councils of the state as a legislator.... He was a patriot, chivalrous and honorable."[5] A scholar of Southwest Virginia history calls Campbell the "Father of Washington County," because of his intelligent and active leadership in settling that region[6]; Tennessee named one of its counties in his honor.[7]

Samuel Cole Williams, another authority on the Old Southwest, maintains Campbell was the best informed man of his time on affairs in Kentucky and Tennessee. Fluent in conversation, he was capable of entertaining the most intelligent of men.[8] Firm and positive in action, Campbell completely disregarded the ordinary means of acquiring popularity, and "though he had some bitter enemies, he could count some of the first men of the age among

1

his personal friends."[9] In physical appearance Campbell had red hair, like many Virginians of his day.[10]

> [N]ot quite six feet [tall], his person was good, his gait erect and lofty, his manners very graceful. His fine eyes, long chin and nose, and general outline of his face would strike the observer in a moment, and impress upon him that he was looking upon no ordinary man. He was pleasant in his manners when he chose to be so, but these traits were not natural to him.[11]

Arthur Campbell's ancestry can be traced back to Dugal Campbell of Scotland and the era of Queen Elizabeth I.[12] The early Stuarts encouraged Scots to emigrate to Ireland in the hope that they could be used to force the Irish to submit to English rule. By 1640 the number taking advantage of the King's offer of land reached a hundred thousand and the number continued to increase throughout the seventeenth century. England also encouraged the emigration of its own people as a cure for its population problem, and thousands of Protestant families settled in Ireland. The Campbells were among the Scots who emigrated to Ireland. John Campbell, grandfather of Arthur, was born near Londonderry in 1674.[13]

The Catholics of Ireland massacred hundreds of the Protestant settlers and forced hundreds more to flee back to the poverty from which they came. As Marcus Lee Hansen has noted, "only the Scots seemed to thrive. For the next century Ulster was a colony of Scotland, serving as a training school for a race of pioneers who were to perform hardier exploits beyond the Atlantic."[14] These were the men who took up arms in defense of William of Orange during the Revolution of 1688 and who withstood the siege of Londonderry in 1689.

After such heroic feats and demonstration of loyalty to the Crown, the Scots of Ulster naturally expected some consideration by the English government, or at least, to be left alone. Neither, as it turned out, came to pass. Having seen two religious wars in one generation, they were now to feel the effects of English commercial policies designed to favor England at Ireland's expense, be it Scots or Irish who felt the effect. It was English economic policies more than any other factor which created conditions resulting in the wave of immigrants pouring into the English colonies in America throughout the eighteenth century.[15]

After the Glorious Revolution of 1688 there was a strong migration of Scots-Presbyterians to Ulster, where land was offered for long term at low rent. By 1715 it was estimated that no fewer than 50,000 Scottish families had settled there since the Revolution. By 1717 the leases began to expire and landlords began to double, even triple, the rent. High rent in addition to resentment over tithes required for the support of the Established Church of England, crop failures in 1714–1717, and the commercial legislation of England which destroyed Irish industry, created an intolerable economic situation. The economic condition together with the Penal Act of 1704 excluding Presbyterians from all civil and military offices, and the prohibiting of Presbyterian ministers from celebrating marriages, were the factors which motivated thousands of Scotch-Irish to escape to the New World.[16]

The Scotch-Irish immigrated to the American colonies in five great waves—1717–1718, 1725–1729, 1740–1741, 1754–1755, and 1771–1775. Some came to the Berkshires and the New Hampshire hills and others to the Mohawk and Cherry valleys of New York. The majority, however, settled in Pennsylvania, usually going beyond the German frontier, occupying the country from Lancaster to Bedford, the Juniata Valley and Redstone country.[17]

Among the Scotch-Irish who arrived with the second great wave of immigrants was John Campbell, grandfather of Arthur Campbell and great-grandfather of William Campbell of Kings Mountain fame. In 1726 John Campbell came with his wife, Grace Hay, and their six sons and three daughters to Sweet Ara in Lancaster, Pennsylvania.[18] Arthur Campbell's father, David, the youngest son of John Campbell, was twenty years of age when he arrived in America. David was a large stout man with silken yellow hair, fair skin, blue eyes, and a "remarkable ... evenness of temper,"[19] a characteristic that would not be found in Arthur.

The Campbells, like hundreds of other families, soon left Pennsylvania. In 1730 John Campbell purchased a tract of land in what was to become Orange County, later Augusta County, Virginia. In 1733 he moved there, just one year after John Lewis, another important pioneer, settled in the same area.[20] Joseph A. Waddell, in his

Annals of Augusta County, presents an interesting description of the movement into the frontier of western Virginia at the time Arthur Campbell's father arrived.

> There was, of course, no road, and for the first comers, no path to guide their steps, except perhaps, the trail of the Indian or buffalo. At night they rested on the ground, with no roof over them but the broad expanse of heaven. After selecting a spot for a night's bivouac, and tethering their horse, fire was kindled by means of flint and steel, and a frugal meal was prepared. . . . Before lying down to rest, many of them did not omit to worship the God of their fathers and invoke His guidance and protection. . . . It was impossible to bring wagons, and all their effects were transported on horseback. . . . Clothing, some bedding, guns and ammunition, a few cooking utensils, seed, corn, axes, saws, etc., and the Bible were indispensable, and were transported at whatever cost of time and labor. The settlers were almost exclusively of the Scot-Irish race, natives of the north of Ireland, but of Scottish ancestry. . . . Most of those who came during the first three or four decades were Dissenters from the Church of England and of the Presbyterian faith.[21]

So great was the number of people settling along the Shenandoah and other rivers on the northwest side of the Blue Ridge Mountains that in 1738 the Virginia Assembly provided for the creation of Augusta and Frederick counties from Orange County. Augusta County government was organized seven years later, the first county court being held at Staunton, December 9, 1745.[22]

Two years after the Campbells came to Virginia, David married Mary Hamilton, "a very intelligent and ambitious little black eyed woman."[23] The Campbells and Hamiltons had for years been close friends. Both families traced their ancestry back to Scotland, and both had come to America aboard the same ship.[24] With his wife Mary, David settled down on his farm where they raised their family and, like hundreds of other families, faced the hardships and dangers of frontier life. By 1741 the couple already had four children, three daughters and a son. John, born in 1741, played an important role in the settling of Southwest Virginia. In 1765, he accompanied Thomas Walker in the exploration of the western wilderness and was one of the first settlers along the Holston River in Southwest Virginia. In July, 1776, he was second in command at the Battle of

Long Island on the Holston and served in many other military campaigns during the Revolution, among them Kings Mountain. He was the father of Governor David Campbell of Virginia.[25]

Arthur, the second son of David and Mary Campbell, was born November 3, 1743, in Augusta County.[26] Here on his father's farm he grew up with his six brothers and six sisters: John, already mentioned, James, William, David, Robert, Patrick, Catherine, Mary, Martha, Margaret, Sarah and Anne. Catherine, born in 1736, married Elijah McLannahan and died in 1798. Mary, born in 1737, married William Lockhart, and Margaret married David Campbell of Campbell's Station, Tennessee. Anne married Archibald Roane, the first teacher at Liberty Hall Academy in Rockbridge County, a judge of the Supreme Court of Tennessee and governor of Tennessee.[27]

Arthur's father had little ambition to make his sons anything more than farmers, and the boys worked long and hard on the land. Their mother had other ideas and saw to it that they were well educated. What their father lacked in means to accomplish this she made up for with the savings of her dowry. Consequently, all the boys received good educations in English and mathematics. David Campbell went to college and became a lawyer in Tennessee, a federal judge in the Tennessee territory, and later a judge of the Supreme Court of Tennessee. He died in 1812 at the age of 62, before he could assume the position of federal judge in the territory of what later became the state of Alabama. Robert Campbell, born in 1752, was a volunteer in an important Indian expedition in 1774, was in the Battle of Long Island Flats on the Holston in 1776, and was in William Christian's Indian campaign in October, 1776. He was a magistrate in Washington County for over 30 years and died in Knoxville, Tennessee, in 1831. Patrick the youngest son was in the Battle of Kings Mountain. He inherited his father's estate but later moved to Williamson County, Tennessee, where he died around the age of 80. Arthur's two other brothers, James and William died in their youth.[28]

Just where Arthur received his early education is uncertain. He and his younger brothers were probably taught by the same man who taught his older brother. John received a good English education, completing his studies under an Irishman, David Robinson, who conducted a private school with a high reputation.[29] There was ample opportunity for schooling. At least 13 English schools existed in Augusta, Rockbridge and Rockingham Counties prior to 1765. As early as 1743, William Wright, a school master, appears on the records of Augusta County. In that year he was teaching on Linville Creek. Another teacher, Samuel Vance, came to the county in 1744. Three years later, Robert Alexander founded a classical school near Greenville, the genesis of Washington and Lee University at Lexington. Others who could have taught the Campbell boys were the Reverend John Craig and James Anderson.[30] Records suggest that Arthur could read by the age of 15[31] and that during the French and Indian War he was taught by the Jesuit Fathers while a prisoner at Detroit, thus receiving a better education than the average boy on the frontier.[32] After the war, Arthur attended Augusta Academy,[33] and it was probably during this time that he was trained as a surveyor and a lawyer.[34]

More important than any formal education, however, Arthur soon learned the skills of a woodsman, how to hunt and to defend himself against the Indians, and in a few short years from the day of his birth, survival would require that he use such skills. He was only 12 at the time of Braddock's Defeat, yet he would be directly involved in the French and Indian War and nowhere was the war more bloody than along the Virginia frontier.

By the middle of the eighteenth century there were 13 separate English colonies in North America. The colonies had been established by different people and for different reasons, with little or no sense of unity or affection toward each other. Most of the population of approximately a quarter of a million lived along the Atlantic coast, with a few pioneers having ventured to the Blue Ridge, and fewer still crossing the Appalachians. Across the Appalachians, west to the Mississippi River and beyond, and from Canada to New Orleans lay New France. The eighty thousand French inhabitants were scattered about this immense region in forts and fur trading posts.

Prior to the 1750s, there had been three major wars between England and France within roughly 50 years. These conflicts did not originate in the English colonies, nor did they have much impact on the colonies after the wars were over and the treaties were signed. However, the war that broke out in 1754, the French and Indian War, was different. It originated in America over conflicting claims in the trans–Appalachian region, specifically the Ohio Valley, and the consequences of this war were profound.

The colony of Virginia, under her charter of 1609, claimed much of New France, including the Ohio Valley, and in 1749, Governor Robert Dinwiddie granted two hundred thousand acres at the forks of the Ohio to a group of land speculators known as the Ohio Company. In 1750, the company sent a North Carolina surveyor, Christopher Gist, across the mountains to survey the grant in preparation for the selling and settlement of the valley. Alarmed over the intrusion into their own claims, the French began constructing forts in preparation for war.

When it became obvious France would challenge Virginia's claim to the Ohio, Governor Dinwiddie, himself a member of the Ohio Company, sent 21 year old George Washington across the mountains to order the French to withdraw. At Fort Le Boeuf, Washington informed the French commandant, Legardere de St. Pierre, that "the lands upon the River Ohio . . . are so notoriously known to be the property of the Crown of Great Britain that it is a matter of equal concern and surprise . . . to hear that a body of French forces are erecting fortresses . . . within his Majesty's dominions." However, to the ultimatum to withdraw, the commandant replied, ". . .I do not think myself obliged to obey it."[35]

Responding to the challenge, Dinwiddie ordered the construction of a fort at the forks of the Ohio, but the French drove the Virginians out and erected Fort Duquesne. Washington then attacked and defeated a small detachment of French troops, and quickly constructed Fort Necessity at Great Meadows. Here on July 4, 1754, Washington surrendered to French forces, but he and his men were allowed to withdraw back across the mountains.

During this same time, delegates from New England, New York, Maryland and Pennsylvania met at Albany at the request of the British government to devise a plan for dealing with the Indians. Benjamin Franklin of Pennsylvania, presented a "Plan of Union" to the Albany Congress, a plan which provided for a union of all the colonies. There would be a grand colonial council of representatives chosen by the colonial assemblies, and a president-general appointed by the Crown. The plan would give the council and president-general control over Indian affairs, the public lands, and the authority to raise an army and navy. For numerous reasons, including the colonial assemblies' fear of losing their authority and the opposition of land speculators, none of the colonies accepted the plan. The Crown appeared to be equally cool toward the Plan of Union.[36]

The failure of the Albany Plan revealed how divided the colonies were, and it also convinced England that it would require British regulars and British money to gain control of the Ohio country. For this purpose the British government sent to American Major-General Edward Braddock with the 44th and 48th regiments of Royal troops. To support the regulars, the Virginia Assembly enacted a draft law giving the justices of the peace of each county the authority to enlist into service all able-bodied men who were not engaged in any lawful employment or who did not have sufficient support and maintenance. Those who could vote in the election of a Burgess were exempt from the draft, as were indentured servants and those under 21 or over 50. In addition to the draftees, two regiments of volunteer militia from Virginia joined Braddock.[37]

Early in June, 1755, Braddock started for Fort Duquesne with some two thousand men including Washington and a few hundred Virginia militia. By July 9, they were within ten miles of their destination, but totally oblivious to the fact that lurking in the woods around them were two hundred Frenchmen and their Indian allies. It was past noon on a bright summer day as the "scarlet columns" of British soldiers kept step to the beat of the drummers. As Francis Parkman described the scene:

> With steady and well-ordered march, the troops advanced into the great labyrinth of woods.... Rank after rank vanished from sight. The forest swallowed them up, and the silence of the wilderness sank down once more on the shores and waters on the Monongahela.[38]

When the British were completely surrounded, the enemy opened fire. The road became a slaughter pen as the French and Indians, hiding behind rocks and trees, fired into the British soldiers, huddled together "like a flock of sheep." After having five horses shot out from under him, General Braddock himself was killed, while Washington rode through the tumult apparently "calm and undaunted," even though two horses were shot from under him and four bullets pierced his clothing. The bloody battle lasted for three hours and when it was over, more than half of Braddock's men, including many Virginians were dead. The survivors fled back across the mountains.[39]

The slaughter on Braddock's Field was slight in comparison to subsequent events resulting from the defeat. The Indian tribes which had been neutral or wavering between the French and British now moved to the side of the French. "The defeat of Braddock," wrote Parkman, "was a signal for the western savages to snatch their tomahawks and assail the English settlements with one accord, murdering and pillaging with ruthless fury, and turning the frontier of Pennsylvania and Virginia into one wide scene of havoc and desolation."[40]

The main method of defense employed by the militia was the establishment of a line of forts and block houses along the frontier occupied by militiamen. Companies of Rangers were organized as separate units from the rest of the militia, to be utilized wherever the governor might direct, but not incorporated with British regulars or to be called on to serve outside the colony.[41] All this was totally insufficient to protect the settlers, both because of the vastness of the territory to be protected and the lack of discipline in the militia. Consequently, the incursions of the Indians became more frequent and bold, extending so far into the settlements that there was fear that the Indians would strike east of the Blue Ridge.

In 1758, a band of Shawanee went to Seyert's Fort about 50 miles from Staunton. The Indians informed the whites that if they gave up the fort their lives would be spared. Fearful that they could not hold it anyway, the whites surrendered, 30 in all. Ten of the prisoners were taken from the fort while the others were tied hand and foot and seated on a log. Standing behind each of the whites stood a Shawanee and when the signal was given they sank their tomahawks into the skulls of their victims. Such was the fate of these prisoners.[42]

On another occasion, a party of warriors with three white men prisoners were returning to their camp when the prisoners attempted to escape. Two of the men were then tied to trees and fires were built around them. Here they remained for some time, gradually being burned to death. After the Indians had enjoyed the writhing agony for a while one stepped up to the dying men, ripped open their bodies and threw their intestines into the flames. Others took their knives, burning sticks and heated irons and pierced and tore the flesh from their victims until death brought an end to their suffering.

The third man was spared for a few hours so that a different method of torture could be inflicted upon him. A hole was dug deep enough that his body could be placed in a standing position in it, with only his head exposed. After his arms had been pinioned to his body, dirt was packed tightly around him. The poor man was then scalped and permitted to remain in that situation for several hours. A fire was then built near his head. The victim soon cried out that his brains were boiling in his skull and he pleaded for instant death. The pleas fell on deaf ears for the Indians continued to allow him to suffer until his eyes burst from their sockets and death put an end to his torment.[43] Such acts of inhumanity as these were also committed by whites. Many a peaceful Indian was murdered by an ignorant, unthinking or self-seeking white for no other reason than to take the Indian's land.

This was the situation on the frontier as Arthur Campbell was growing into manhood. He was well aware of the horrors of Indian warfare when he joined a company of Rangers on September 14, 1758, under the command of Captain John Dickenson.[44] The company was stationed at Fort Young, which was located about 60 miles southwest of Staunton on the Jackson River.[45] Washington often wrote of the weaknesses of the frontier forts and Alexander S. Withers has noted in particular, the weakness of Fort Young.[46] The fort was soon attacked by Wyandottes who divided into parties, striking at different places in Augusta County. At the time of the attack on Fort Young, Campbell, not quite 15 years old, had gone with a party of men some distance from the fort in search of plums. When the Indians struck, Campbell was in a plum tree and a bullet grazed his knee. He jumped to the ground, but the shock of landing on his wounded knee prevented him from escaping with the others. The Wyandottes were from the vicinity of Detroit and they immediately set out for that country. Campbell was loaded with packs and forced to march for seven days. When he became exhausted and unable to travel, he was treated with great severity. He realized his fate might be the same as so many other prisoners, and this would probably have been the case had it not been for an aged chief who intervened, protecting him from further injury. When the party reached the Indian towns, the chief adopted him into his family.

On the way to Detroit the party stopped at Sunyendeaned, a Wyandotte town, located on a small creek which emptied into Little Lake below the mouth of the Sandusky. There Campbell met another prisoner, James Smith, who was captured in the spring of 1755. Campbell passed the time by reading Smith's Bible. Reading the passage: "It is good for a man that he bear the yoke in his youth," Campbell remarked to Smith that "they ought to be resigned to the will of Providence, as they were now bearing the yoke in their youth."[47]

When Campbell was taken to Detroit, he turned his attention to the study of the Indians, their character, language and customs and he wisely applied what he learned. His red hair was plucked out, and when it grew back it was dyed black, apparently styled in Indian fashion. With such enthusiasm for Indian ways he soon acquired the confidence of the tribe. He and the chief hunted all over the territory later to become the states of Michigan, Ohio, Indiana, and Illinois. The Jesuit Fathers at Detroit were also impressed with the bright English boy and they took time to teach him.

For the English, the war began as a series of disasters, but slowly shifted after William Pitt became prime minister in 1758, the year Louisbourg, Fort Frontenac and Duquesne were captured by the British. These victories were followed up in 1759 and 1760 by the fall of Quebec and Montreal.

In the fall of 1760 word came to the Wyandotte towns that the British were marching toward Lake Erie. Campbell decided that, although the British were still several hundred miles away, he would attempt to escape. Success required skill and determination, for it would be extremely difficult, and if caught he could lose his life. His chance came when he joined a hunting party, which, after several days separated, each to hunt on his own. Once on his own, he set out in the general direction of the British troops. In two weeks he traveled two hundred miles through unknown country, narrowly avoiding Indian hunting parties, and living off whatever he was able to find. At Presqu'Isle he met Major Robert Rogers of the British Rangers and related to him his experience as a prisoner and his subsequent escape. Because of Campbell's knowledge of the territory, Rogers requested that he guide the army to Detroit, where on December 25, 1760, Campbell witnessed the surrender of the French fort.[48]

The French and Indian War was officially concluded with the signing of the Treaty of Paris of 1763. France was forced to cede to England all of the territory of New France east of the Mississippi River and Canada. French claims west of the Mississippi and New Orleans were relinquished to Spain as compensation for Spain's loss of Florida to England. Thus, England emerged from the war triumphant, its empire greatly enlarged, while France lost all her possessions on the mainland of North America.

Campbell's parents had heard nothing concerning their son since his captivity and they assumed he was dead. To soothe their feelings, people around them no longer mentioned Arthur's name. One can imagine the Campbells' feelings of happiness when they received a letter from Arthur informing them that he was safe at Pittsburgh and would soon return home. John, his brother, left immediately to meet him. Campbell had changed a great deal during the years of his captivity and his parents hardly recognized him when he first came into view. He had grown tall and erect, with manly steps and the lofty air of an Indian. Family friends came to see him, but their constant questioning annoyed him as he had acquired the taciturnity of the red man.[49]

The war was a turning point in Campbell's life, with rewards and opportunities awaiting him at its conclusion. Not only did he receive 2000 acres of land for his services in the war,[50] but life with the Indians prepared him for the difficult years ahead. From this time on he exhibited those traits of character, which, although often condemned, were absolutely vital for a leader of men on the frontier. His knowledge of the Indians and the Northwest Territory proved to be of great value during the years of the westward movement and the American Revolution.

2 On the Holston

Large land companies like the Ohio Company, the Loyal Company and the Mississippi Company, and pioneer families were at first thrilled at the possibilities opening up to them beyond the mountains, now that the French were no longer a threat. Their hopes were quickly dashed, however, by the Proclamation of 1763, which prohibited the colonists from crossing the crest of the Appalachians. The purpose of the Proclamation, issued by King George III, was to provide a temporary reserve for the Indians in the transappalachian region until treaties could be negotiated with the separate tribes moving them further west. The Treaty of Fort Stanwix with the Iroquois in 1768 opened vast areas of land in western Pennsylvania and Virginia, and in what is now the state of Kentucky. The Treaty of Hard Labor with the Cherokees the same year, extended the Proclamation Line further west from Fort Chiswell in Southwest Virginia to the mouth of the Great Kanawha on the Ohio River. In subsequent treaties, the Creeks and the Cherokees ceded thousands of square miles in Virginia, North and South Carolina and Georgia.[1]

The most forward advance of the westward movement was in Southwest Virginia and western North Carolina. This region consisted of forest-covered mountains and valleys, running from northeast to southwest. On the western side lay the Cumberland Mountains and on the eastern, the Great Smoky Mountains. In the valley were the streams of the Clinch, Holston, Watauga, Nolichucky and French Broad, which together formed the Tennessee River.

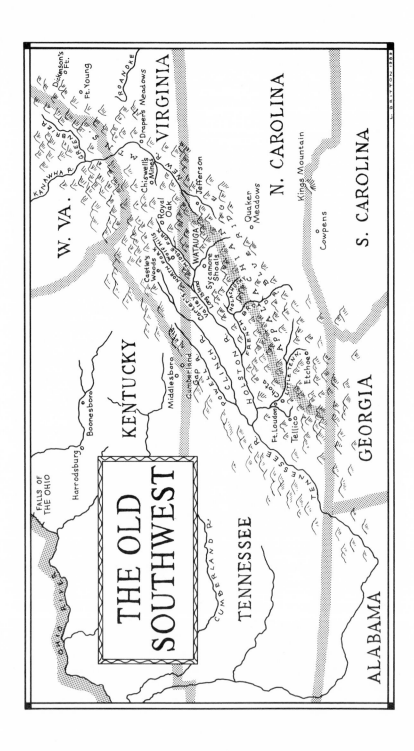

THE OLD SOUTHWEST

L. BRITTON 1983

Following the French and Indian War, pioneers moved into this region, settling on the banks of the Holston and Watauga Rivers. Most of the early pioneers came from Virginia and North Carolina, and were, as Theodore Roosevelt so well described them, "a sturdy race, enterprising and intelligent, fond of the strong excitement inherent in the adventurous frontier life." Wrote Roosevelt, "Their untamed and turbulent passions, and the lawless freedom of their lives, made them a population very productive of wild, headstrong characters...."[2]

In 1769, the same year that Daniel Boone first went to Kentucky, and one year before James Robertson of North Carolina explored the Watauga Valley, Arthur Campbell's brother, John, purchased 740 acres of land on the Middle Fork of the Holston River. The next year, Arthur accompanied him to Southwest Virginia. Arthur obtained 240 acres of the 740 acre tract, located one mile east of what became the town of Marion, Virginia. Here on what was called "Royal Oak," they built a cabin in full view of the Holston and Blue Ridge and the following year the rest of the Campbell family joined them.[3]

About this same time, other future leaders on the frontier settled in the region. William Russell built his home in the Clinch Valley at "Castle's Woods." William Preston moved from Staunton to an estate called "Smithfield" at the site of Old Draper's Meadows, and the Shelbys—Evan, Isaac and John—came to the Holston. William Campbell moved from Augusta County to Aspenvale, near the present site of Seven Mile Ford, located between Marion and Abingdon. William Christian moved to the area and further south and west on the Watauga River and in Carter's Valley could be found James Robertson, the "Father of Tennessee," John Carter, William Bean, and John Sevier.[4] These were real frontiersmen, living on the westernmost fringe of the colonies, an area which was so important during the Revolution and in the exploration of Kentucky. These pioneers showed their independent spirit from the outset as they not only defied the Indians in moving to the Holston and Watauga, but also George III and the colonial governors. Disregarding the Proclamation Line and Indian treaties, they took over whatever land they wanted.

Augusta County, formed in 1738, took in all of western Virginia, an area too large to be properly governed. With the population of the Holston region expanding, and because of the inconvenience of doing business at the county seat at Staunton, Botetourt County was created from Augusta in November, 1769. From the beginning of Botetourt County it was realized that within a short time another county would be needed in order to provide for the needs of the inhabitants. The act establishing Botetourt, therefore, specified that because the people situated on the waters of the Mississippi would be so remote from the county seat, another county would be formed as soon as sufficient numbers warranted that action.[5] In 1772, the Virginia General Assembly created Fincastle County out of Botetourt.[6] Campbell's home at Royal Oak was located in Botetourt County, but after the creation of Fincastle, it lay within the bounds of that county.

Campbell was at this time a typical farmer on the frontier, and had married his first cousin, Margaret Campbell, "a woman of excellent mind and of uncommon beauty and sprightliness."[7] It was she who pushed Arthur forward in his efforts for distinction as a public figure. "Her whole mind seemed to be devoted to this one object, to which she made every other bend. No privation, however great . . . annoyed her if she believed it was in consequence of her husband's efforts to acquire either military or civil distinction." Campbell must have been the envy of every man if his wife really was "the most exemplary of women in her deportment toward [him], never having a thought in opposition to his upon any subject, and believing him to be the greatest man in the country."[8]

Although Campbell never became the greatest man in the country, Margaret must have been extremely pleased at her husband's rapid rise to distinction, both as a military officer and civic leader. Perhaps it was more than a coincidence that this rise began about the time he married Margaret. He was at the time a captain in the militia and a justice of the peace in Fincastle County.

The first session of the Fincastle County Court was held at the Lead Mines on the New River, January 5, 1773. Members of the court included Arthur Campbell, William Preston, William Christian, Walter Crockett, James Thompson, William Inglis, Stephen Trigg, and James McGavock. Campbell was the first to be sworn into office.[9]

You shall swear that as a justice of the peace in the county of Fincastle in all articles in the commission to you directed, you shall do equal right to the poor and to the rich, after your cunning, wit and power, according to law; and you shall not be of any counsel of any quarrel hanging before you, and the issues, fines and amercements that shall happen to be made, and all the forfeitures which shall fall before you, you shall cause to be entered, without any concealment or embezzling; you shall not let for gift or other causes but will and truly you shall do your office of justice of the peace, as well within your county court as without; and you shall not take any gift, fee or gratuity, for anything to be done by virtue of your office and you shall not direct or cause to be directed any warrant by you to be made to the parties, and you shall direct them to the sheriff, or bailiffs or said county, or other the King's officers or ministers, or other indifferent persons, to do execution thereof, so help you God.[10]

The office of justice of the peace was a position of dignity and was usually held by men of influence and ability. Few of the justices were learned in law and many probably had little education. But the cases concerning the county court, though often tedious, did not usually involve complicated points of law, and as the oath indicated, sound judgment and common sense were all that were required in handing out justice. Justices were commissioned by the governor for an indefinite period, which usually turned out to be for life. The number of justices on the court varied from about eight to eighteen.[11] They were very irregular in attendance at court and as a rule more than half of them were absent at every session.[12] Later in his career Campbell was criticized for his laxness in attending.

The first sessions of the Fincastle County Court turned much of its attention to the opening of roads. Prior to this time the settlers usually followed Indian and buffalo trails or traveled by canoe. Another important item was the granting of permission to erect grist mills. Before mills were built the individual settler cracked his own corn if he wanted meal or flour. On March 13, 1770, the Botetourt County Court had granted Campbell permission to build a grist mill and this was the only mill on the Holston and Clinch rivers until 1773.[13] The importance of Campbell's mill was recognized by the court, which ordered that roads be built to the mill to make it more accessible.[14]

Court was held at the county seat and court days were holidays for the inhabitants. On court days one could observe settlers coming on horseback or wagons from every direction. On the courthouse green could be found every class of people, the hunter and backwoodsman, the small land owner and the grand proprietor. They came not only concerned with the business of the court but to conduct their own private business, to settle old debts and acquire new ones. There were auctions, transfers of property, stump-preaching and politicking.[15]

Because of the importance of the county seat there was often much disagreement as to where it should be located, and the acts creating new counties usually specified the inconvenience of the inhabitants in doing business at the county seat as a reason to create new ones. On the second day of the Fincastle Court it was recommended to the governor that the courthouse be built on McCall's place instead of the Lead Mines where the court was presently in session. The reasons given were that McCall's was more centrally located and in an area where there were good lands and meadows. The Lead Mines it was pointed out, were near the southern boundary of the county, and off the leading road. Campbell was opposed to the request and while there is no evidence to show that it was because of his opposition, Governor Dunmore never agreed to the request and the Lead Mines continued to be the site of the county seat.[16]

While county government was developing in Southwest Virginia, the smoldering hostility of the northern tribes over the Treaty of Fort Stanwix came to the surface. The Miamis, Shawnee, Delawares, Wyandottes and Mingoes never accepted the terms of the Treaty of 1768. In 1770 the Shawnee and Delawares united hoping at last to block the advance of the white man. In 1771, at a congress on the banks of the Scioto River, they brought other tribes into a great Northwest Confederacy, one of the most powerful Indian forces that ever threatened the frontier. At the head of the Confederacy was the famous Shawnee chief, Cornstalk. Cornstalk had fought against the English in the French and Indian War and during Pontiac's uprising, following the close of the war, he raided the Greenbriar settlements in western Virginia. Though he was friendly to the whites from 1764 to 1774, growing friction between the two races forced him to take to the war path in 1774, when he led his warriors against Colonel Andrew Lewis at Point Pleasant, in what became known as Dunmore's War.[17]

While the Indians were preparing to defend their country, surveyors and land speculators were beginning the invasion of the Kentucky country. In April, 1774, William Preston sent John Floyd, his deputy surveyor in Fincastle, to the Ohio River to survey land for veterans of the French and Indian War. Among the first surveys made in Kentucky was one of 1000 acres at the Falls of the Ohio for Arthur Campbell.[18] Surveys were also made for Preston, Patrick Henry, William Byrd III, Thomas Walker, John May, William Fleming, Andrew Lewis, William Christian and George Washington.[19]

It was the familiar story of white intrusion into Indian lands that brought on Dunmore's War in the summer of 1774. The immediate cause, however, was the rash of isolated murders inflicted on each race by the other. The most significant was the murder of the family of a Mingo chief whose English name was John Logan. This occurred on Yellow Creek in Ohio, April 20, 1774. Three white men by the names of Greathouse, Sapperton and King lured into their fur-trading post 12 Indians, including a woman with a baby. After getting the Indians drunk the white men murdered them. Only the baby was spared. One of the Indian braves was Logan's brother; the woman with the baby was his sister.[20] Although Logan may not have been a chief, he occupied a position of importance among the Mingoes on the Ohio and Scioto Rivers. He had been friendly toward the whites until the murder of his family.[21]

Reprisals led to reprisals and soon the frontiers of Pennsylvania and Virginia were ablaze. On May 6, Valentine Crawford wrote Colonel George Washington from Pennsylvania concerning the murder of Logan's family: "It has ruined all the settlements west of the Monongahela. There were more than one thousand people crossing the river going eastward in a single day."[22] Two days later, Valentine's brother, Colonel William Crawford, wrote Washington that "our inhabitants are much alarmed, many hundreds having gone eastward over the Allegheny Mountains and the whole country is vacated as far as the Monongahela."[23]

On June 10, the governor of Virginia, Dunmore, sent word to the county lieutenants of the frontier counties that news from Fort

Pitt had given him good reason to doubt any chance of peace with the Indians. The governor believed that force was the only way to stop them. He ordered the county lieutenants to prepare the militia to defend their own counties and to be ready to march to the assistance of others. The county lieutenant of Fincastle was William Preston, who was born in Ireland in 1729 and immigrated to Augusta County, Virginia, in his early youth. Preston was a captain in the Sandy Creek expedition of 1756 and later deputy surveyor and sheriff of Augusta until he moved to Botetourt in 1767. He held similar offices in Botetourt, and in 1773 was appointed surveyor and county lieutenant of Fincastle.[24]

Southwest Virginia was in a most vulnerable position, situated as it was between the northern tribes now on the warpath and the Cherokees to the south threatening to take the same path. In late June, 1774, Campbell, who now held the rank of major, and was responsible for the defense of the southern part of Fincastle County, wrote the county lieutenant that the inhabitants of the lower settlements on the Watauga were greatly alarmed and were preparing to leave the area. Here again it was the familiar story of the senseless murder of an Indian, this time a Cherokee, that created the anxiety. Campbell was doubtful the suspected murderer, by the name of Crabtree, would be brought to justice. Campbell believed it would be easier to find two hundred men to protect Crabtree from the law than ten who would bring him to justice.[25]

A great deal of responsibility now rested with Campbell who was directly concerned with the explosive Cherokee situation. Any overt action which might appear hostile to the Cherokees could cause them to take the warpath, while no action at all might be interpreted as weakness and invite an attack. His approach was one of preparation and diplomacy. Campbell ordered Evan Shelby to keep his eyes on the Cherokees and to notify him immediately at the first sign of hostilities.[26] At the same time he suggested that Colonel Andrew Lewis write a letter to one of the chiefs, Oconostota, whom Lewis had known for a long time, to smooth things over between the Indians and whites.[27] Oconostota lived at Great Echota, the Overhill Cherokee town. He had supported the English in the French and Indian War until alienated by the treatment shown the Cherokee warriors by Virginians on the frontier; he was also unhappy over the treatment he received at the hands of South Carolina officials. During the attack on Fort Prince George in 1760, it was he who gave the signal to shoot down Lieutenant Cotymore when the officer came out of the fort to talk peace. Later Oconostota was responsible for the massacre of the defenders of Fort Loudoun after they surrendered.[28]

Campbell also wrote to Alexander Cameron, the deputy commissioner of Indian affairs, asking Cameron to use his influence with the Cherokees to keep the peace.[29] Spies were sent out to observe Indian paths and militia officers were ordered to keep Campbell advised on the situation in the lower settlements.[30] Fortunately, Campbell's measures paid off for he received information from the Little Carpenter (Attakullaculla), the noted Cherokee chief, that the Cherokees would not go to war provided they were not further provoked.[31] Despite Campbell's effort and the Little Carpenter's inclination toward peace, Crabtree remained free to harass and murder peaceful Indians. Campbell lamented to Preston: "It appears that Crabtree and a few misled followers will frustrate all we can do."[32]

While these problems were developing with the Cherokees, Dunmore was preparing for an expedition against the northern tribes. There were to be two armies, one under Governor Dunmore and the other under Colonel Andrew Lewis, county lieutenant of Botetourt. Campbell played an important part in organizing the troops under Lewis and supplying them, partly at his own expense. One of his most difficult problems, always a concern on the frontier, was how to deal with jealousy among the men regarding the command of individual companies going on the expedition. On August 12, Campbell informed Preston that he was sorry to find so many officers forming companies. One of William Campbell's men by the name of Vance had, in effect, stopped the men in one company from going with Captain Russell, and Joseph Drake had formed a company using some of Captain William Campbell's men. Campbell complained to Preston that when he attempted to put an end to such irregular procedures, Drake became belligerent and ten men refused to go on the expedition without Drake as their officer.[33] Even Shelby's company had to be divided in order to make a place for William Cocke, who, after all this trouble, ended up staying at home. When Captain David Long attempted to organize a company of Watauga men, Preston found it necessary to warn him not to get his men from Shelby's or William Campbell's company.[34] These obstacles and the problem of obtaining supplies were finally overcome and the expedition got under way.

To the south, rumors circulated that the Cherokees had killed white traders and were preparing for war. It did not help matters that there were 40 Shawnee in the Cherokee towns willing to join them in an attack on the settlements.[35] To meet this threat, militia captains were ordered to draft and hold in readiness enough men to defend the settlements.[36] July and August passed, however, without serious threat and Campbell was convinced that Lewis' expedition held the key to peace on the Holston. If Lewis failed, the Cherokees would probably join the northern tribes and destroy the frontier settlements. On the other hand, Campbell thought that if Lewis succeeded, the Cherokees would realize that they alone could not drive out the whites, and would, therefore, seek peace.

All during the month of September there were attacks on isolated settlements, with families being massacred. On September 25, 1774, news reached Campbell that the Cherokees had struck the day before at two different points on the Holston. Two blacks were captured below Castle's Woods at Moore's Fort and a considerable number of horses and cattle were taken. On Reedy Creek, 40 miles south at Watauga, John Roberts' house was attacked. Roberts, his wife and three children were scalped and a boy taken prisoner. A small boy who received a blow on the head from a tomahawk survived and was taken to Campbell's house. The boy's injury did not appear too serious for he could talk sensibly. "For my part," wrote Campbell, "I don't know as I ever had tenderer feelings of compassion for any human species. . . ." He sent for an old man who had some medical skills and he asked William Preston to send a doctor, and if the doctor could not come, to have some medicine sent up.[37] Despite Campbell's efforts, the little boy died, lamenting to the last that he had not been "able to fight enough to save his mammy."[38]

When it appeared that there would be an Indian war, many of the inhabitants began to flee eastward to safety. This had the effect of weakening defense efforts. Campbell had the difficult task of preventing such an exodus. To encourage the inhabitants to remain on the frontier he built forts on the Holston and Clinch rivers and took other measures for the protection of the inhabitants. He was hampered, however, by the constant problem of lack of ammunition and he advised Preston that he must be supplied if he were to defend the country.[39]

Campbell was doubtful that the Cherokees were responsible for all the murders on the Holston, although a few young braves from the Cherokee Nation undoubtedly had made raids on the settlements. In October a black woman who escaped from a raiding party described one of her captors. Campbell was convinced that it was Chief Logan. Her report added credence to a note that had been found at the home of a man named Roberts, mistakenly blaming Captain Michael Cressap for the murder of Logan's family and signed, "Captain John Logan."[40] By the middle of October, Logan apparently had satisfied his vengeance and returned to his home in the North. About this time news reached the Holston that Colonel Lewis had won a major victory at Point Pleasant. Cornstalk sued for peace and the Treaty of Camp Charlotte, opening the Ohio territory to settlement, was signed. Cornstalk kept the promises of peace he made at Camp Charlotte in 1774 and at Fort Pitt the following year, but despite this fact he would later be senselessly murdered by whites who viewed all Indians as enemies.[41] Logan, who pointed out that he was a warrior and not a councilor, did not attend the peace negotiations in 1774, and it was only after Major William Crawford destroyed the Mingo towns that peace with this tribe was obtained. To Dunmore, Logan sent the moving message:

> I appeal to any White man to say if ever he entered Logan's cabin hungry and he gave him not meat; if ever he came cold and naked and he clothed him not? During the course of the last long and bloody war, Logan remained idle in his camp, an advocate for peace. Such was my love for the Whites that my countrymen pointed as I passed and said, "Logan is the friend of the White man!" ... Colonel Cresap, the last spring, in cold blood and unprovoked, murdered all the relations of Logan, not even sparing my women and children. There runs not a drop of my blood in the veins of any living creature. This called on me for revenge. I have sought it. I have killed many. I have fully glutted my vengeance.

For my country, I rejoice at the beams of peace; but do not harbor a thought that mine is the joy of fear. Logan never felt fear. He will not turn on his heel to save his life. Who is there to mourn for Logan? Not one![42]

Under Campbell's leadership the southwestern settlements had been protected while many of its best men were away with Lewis at Point Pleasant. His wisdom and skill in dealing with the Cherokees had prevented a war with that nation. Relative peace now came to the frontier of Virginia, and Campbell, sitting on his front porch, could see hundreds of pioneers moving westward along the "Great Road" to Kentucky.[43] It was to be a short peace, however, for in less than a year, fighting commenced between the American colonies and the mother country, and the Indians found an unexpected but welcomed ally.

3 Revolutionary Rumblings

Victory at Point Pleasant on October 10, 1774, temporarily ended the organized raids on the Holston settlements and gave the frontiersmen an opportunity to turn their attention toward another matter of rising importance. During and after the French and Indian War, friction between Britain and the American colonies over colonial policy continued to increase. Considered separately, these points of conflict do not seem significant enough to lead to revolution. Jefferson would make this point later in the Declaration of Independence when he wrote:

> Prudence indeed will dictate that governments long established should not be changed for light and transient causes. . . . But when a long train of abuses and usurpations, pursuing invariably the same object, evinces a design to reduce . . . [the people] under absolute despotism, it is their right, it is their duty, to throw off such government. . . .[1]

This "train of abuses" was well underway by the conclusion of the French and Indian War. Writs of assistance and the "parson's cause" created friction between the colonies and London while the war was still going on. Writs of assistance, which were general search warrants used to catch smugglers, were vigorously denounced. In a fiery speech, James Otis, a Boston lawyer, argued that the writs violated the people's natural rights. The "parson's cause" originated in Virginia after George III disallowed the Two Penny Act which would have reduced the tax required of Virginians for Anglican

25

ministers' salaries. Not content with the royal veto of the Two Penny Act, the clergy sued the Virginia colony for back pay. Patrick Henry defended Virginia in a case which helped make him famous soon afterward. It also intensified opposition to the established Church of England.

The issue of taxation became the most serious conflict between Britain and the colonies. Beginning with the Sugar Act of 1764, the British government began what is referred to as the "New Colonial System," the purpose of which was to tax the colonies. Indeed, the Act of 1764 was entitled the "Revenue Act" and it was the first measure ever passed for the stated purpose of raising revenue. The following year the Stamp Act became a law. The act affected some of the most important and powerful citizens in the colonies, such as lawyers, ministers and journalists, but the cry of "no taxation without representation," a boycott of British goods, the total disregard of the law, and violent opposition forced its repeal in 1766. The Townshend Acts of 1767, placing a duty, or tax, on imports such as lead, glass, and tea, and the setting up in Boston of a Board of Customs Commissioners with all its ramifications, was as equally detestable as the previous tax measures had been. Although the Townshend Acts were repealed in 1770, fist fights between Redcoats and locals and such episodes as the Boston Massacre, when five Bostonians were shot to death by British soldiers, kept the fire smoldering between 1770 and 1773.

The Tea Act of 1773 is a clear example of how the colonists and England misunderstood each other. This measure actually cut the price that Americans paid for tea, while at the same time, it was intended to help keep the British East India Company from going bankrupt. The colonists, however, interpreted it as a trick to get them to pay the small tax on tea carried over from the repealed Townshend Acts, and merchants opposed it for it amounted to granting the British East India Company a monopoly of the tea business. Thus, opposition to the Tea Act of 1773 was immediate and widespread, but opposition was most intense in Boston where the East India tea was actually destroyed as a result of the "Boston Tea Party."

In England, the time had come to punish Massachusetts. A series of measures known as the Coercive Acts were passed by

Parliament, while in America they were called the "Intolerable Acts." One of the bills closed the port of Boston until the British East India Company was compensated for its losses. This measure and the other "intolerable acts" led to the First Continental Congress at Philadelphia.[2]

Virginia had been in the forefront of the colonies in opposition to the Proclamation of 1763, the Stamp Act, and subsequent tax measures, and was the first colony to side with Massachusetts after the passage of the "Intolerable Acts" in 1774. When in 1769 the Burgesses passed resolutions against British taxation policies, the governor, Lord Botetourt, promptly dissolved them. Just as promptly they met again at a private home, chose Peyton Randolph as their chairman, and proceeded to create a nonimportation agreement. The agreement was broadened into an association the following year and a committee of 125 was appointed to see that the association's decisions were observed. In 1773 the Burgesses were dissolved by Governor Dunmore when radical leaders, including Patrick Henry, Thomas Jefferson, and Richard Henry Lee, created a committee of intercolonial correspondence and asked the other colonies to do the same.[3] By 1774 the Burgesses were well experienced in dealing with their governor.

In May of 1774, news of the Boston Port Act arrived in Virginia. Jefferson, Henry Lee and others held a conference and agreed that a day of fasting and prayer should be proclaimed to focus attention on the Act. The Burgesses concurred and June 1 was set as a day of fasting. Dunmore again dissolved them and they responded by meeting at Raleigh Tavern the next day. With Randolph again serving as chairman, they drew up another nonimportation agreement, but more important, they instructed their committees of correspondence to propose an annual continental congress.[4]

The committees of correspondence in New York and Philadelphia had suggested a continental congress a few days before, but it was several days after their own decision that the Virginians received word that other colonies were favorable to such a congress. Hearing this news, 25 of the Burgesses who had not already left for home met on May 30 and issued a call for a convention to meet at Williamsburg on August 1, 1774. The convention met on the appointed day, elected delegates to the First Continental Congress, and devised a more thorough nonimportation agreement. This convention, according to H.J. Eckenrode, marked the actual beginning of the Revolution in Virginia.[5]

The First Continental Congress met in Philadelphia on October 20, 1774. The Congress entered into an association and agreed on a number of articles which, it was believed, would force the British government to change its colonial policy to one more in accord with present American thinking. The primary method to force this change was economic pressure. Among the articles agreed to by the Congress was one stating

> That a committee be chosen in every county, city and town by those who are qualified to vote for representatives in the Legislature, whose business it shall be, attentively to observe the conduct of all persons touching this association, and when it shall be made to appear to the satisfaction of the majority of any such committee, that any person within the limits of their appointment has violated this association, that such majority do forthwith cause the truth of that case to be published in the *Gazette*, to the end that all such foes to the rights of British America may be publicly known, and universally condemned as the enemies of American liberty; and thenceforth we respectively will break off all dealing with him or her.[6]

On January 20, 1775, in compliance with the resolves of the Continental Congress, the freeholders of Fincastle County met at Chiswell's Mines and after approving the Continental Articles of Association elected a committee to see that it was carried out. Proven leaders were chosen: Major Arthur Campbell, his brother David, Colonel William Preston, Colonel William Christian, Captain Stephen Trigg, Major William Inglis, Captain Walter Crockett, Captain John Montgomery, Captain James McGavack, Captain William Campbell, Captain Thomas Madison, Captain Daniel Smith, Captain William Russell, Captain Evan Shelby, Lieutenant William Edmondson, and the Reverend Charles Cummings.[7] The committee elected William Christian as its chairman, and David Campbell was appointed clerk. An address, unanimously agreed to by the people of the county, was sent to the delegates that represented Virginia in Philadelphia.

> Had it not been for our remote situation, and the Indian War which were lately engaged in . . . we would before this time have made known to you our thankfulness for the very important services you have rendered to your country. We heartily concur in your resolutions, and shall, in every instance, strictly and invariably adhere thereto. . . .[8]

The address expressed the sentiments of "a people whose hearts overflowed with love and duty to our lawful sovereign, George III." They were willing to risk their lives, they said, in the service of the King for the support of the Protestant religion and the rights and liberties of his subjects, as they had been established by "compact, law, and ancient charters." They were grieved at the differences which now existed between the colonies and the parent state and ardently wished to see harmony restored.

What were the grievances of these frontier settlers? They responded, in part, out of sympathy for the easterners, but also out of resentment to what they viewed as outside interference in their lives. The frontiersmen expressed "love and duty" in regard to George III, when in fact they had no such feelings at all. Actually, they would support the King and his government as long as such support did not restrict them in any way. Like other colonists, they had reached the stage of maturity where it was increasingly difficult to understand why England had any authority over them at all. Thomas Paine elaborated on this point in *Common Sense*:

> To be always running 3,000 or 4,000 miles [to England] with a tale or a petition, waiting four or five months for an answer, which, when obtained, requires five or six more to explain it in, will in a few years be looked upon as folly and childishness — there was a time when it was proper, and there is a proper time for it to cease.
>
> Small islands not capable of protecting themselves are the proper objects for kingdoms to take under their care; but there is something absurd in supposing a continent to be perpetually governance by an island. In no instance has nature made the satellite larger than its primary planet; and as England and America, with respect to each other, reverses the common order of nature, it is evident that they belong to different systems: England to Europe, America to itself.[9]

The grievances which the frontier people had with the home government were the Proclamation of 1763 and subsequent land policies which prevented them from taking up all the lands they found unoccupied by whites. In their address they pointed out how they had crossed the Atlantic, explored the wilderness and faced the barbarities and depredations of the Indians. These "fatigues and dangers" they patiently bore with the hope of enjoying the rights and liberties which other Virginians had been granted. This had not been the case, they claimed. Even to the remote frontier regions, England, with its unlimited and unconstitutional power, had pursued them, stripping them of that liberty and property which God, nature, and the rights of man, had vested in them.

Although they may have considered independence as a solution to their ills, they were not ready "to shake off our duty or allegiance to our lawful sovereign...," so long as they could "enjoy the free exercise or our religion as Protestants, and our liberties and properties as British subjects." In other words, so long as they had the liberty to do as they pleased in the remote frontier regions. But in no uncertain terms they warned that if their enemies

> attempt to dragoon us out of those inestimable privileges which we are entitled to as subjects, and to reduce us to a state of slavery, we declare that we are deliberately and resolutely determined never to surrender them to any power upon earth, but at the expense of our lives.[10]

These were their "real though unpolished sentiments of loyalty," under which they resolved "to live and die."[11]

Regardless of how many or how few of the charges against the British government were actually true, the significant fact is that the people of Fincastle who were in a position to express their feelings, believed they were true. Thus, they were Patriots. What they really wanted was the political power to determine their own destiny, and for this power they were willing to die.

What if it had been otherwise? What if Fincastle and other frontier counties did not "heartily concur" with the resolutions of Congress and were not willing to support the East once independence was declared? It appears that had frontier leaders such as Campbell, Preston, and others been Loyalists instead of Patriots, it would have been impossible for the American colonies to obtain independence.

As it was, however, the frontier Patriots served as a barrier between the British-Indian alliance in the West and the Patriots in the East. Not only did western support for the Revolution free Tidewater men to serve in the regular army, but the West contributed some of its best men to the eastern armies.

Eckenrode has noted that the Continental Association was carried out rigidly and with great effect in Virginia because of strong local feeling. Each county was "a little world of its own." A small group of prominent men, usually with family ties, organized the opinion in each community.[12] This was certainly true in Fincastle County. In the months following its formation, the County Committee of Safety took action against those who refused to serve in the Patriot militia and those who spoke out against the Committee, or who were suspected of being unfriendly toward the Patriot cause.[13]

John Adams of Massachusetts estimated that about one third of the colonists were Patriots, one third Loyalists and one third were indifferent. The County Committee of Safety's role was decisive in determining which side the back country would take. When some of the back country elite were excluded from power they tended toward the Loyalist side or became neutral.[14] Whether one was a Patriot (Whig) or a Loyalist (Tory) often depended also on the military situation. If British forces were strong in a region, Loyalist sentiment was usually strong. Unlike the situation in Georgia and the Carolinas, the British Army never occupied any of Southwest Virginia, and Loyalist sentiment, although present, was never very strong. When Loyalist sentiment did spring up, as it did from time to time, it was quickly put down by the militia. Arthur Campbell, who was county lieutenant of Washington County, and his cousin William Campbell, were especially vigorous in putting down Loyalists.[15]

In accordance with the recommendations of the Continental Congress, a convention was held at Richmond on March 20, 1775, to examine the whole question of relations between the colonies and the Mother Country. On March 23, the convention took up the proposal of putting the colony into a posture of defense, and it was on this occasion, according to William Wirt, that Patrick Henry made the moving address:

Gentlemen may cry, "Peace! peace! —but there is no peace. The war is actually begun! The next gale that sweeps from the north will bring to our ears the clash of resounding arms! Our brethern are already in the field! Why stand we here idle? What is it that gentlemen wish? What would they have? Is life so dear, or peace so sweet, as to be purchased at the price of chains and slavery? Forbid it. Almighty God! I know not what course others may take, but as for me, give me liberty or give me death!"[16]

Governor Dunmore was alarmed by the actions of the March Convention in providing for the defense of the colony. On April 20, he removed the gunpowder from the magazine at Williamsburg to the *Magdalene*, a man-of-war anchored off Yorktown. Patrick Henry, at the head of hundreds of Virginians, gathered with arms and threatened to retake the powder. To this threat, Dunmore was outwardly bold, declaring: "The whole country can lastly be made a solitude, and by the living God if an insult is offered to me or to those who have obeyed my orders, I will declare freedom to the slaves and lay the town to ashes!"[17] Despite the threats, however, he was compelled to pay for the powder.

Meanwhile, a conciliatory plan which Lord North pushed through Parliament had reached the colonies and Dunmore convened the Burgesses. This plan, which had been submitted by Lord North to the House of Commons on February 20, 1775, proposed that the colonists devise a plan of their own for raising revenue. The revenue would go toward the common defense and as long as such funds were provided, Parliament would refrain from levying any tax on the colonists. This, so it seemed, would pacify those who were constantly asserting "no taxation without representation." As historians Oscar T. Bark and Hugh T. Lefler point out, the plan did not get at the crux of the matter, however, for Parliament maintained its right to tax the colonies and British soldiers would still be stationed in America. Thus, the conciliatory plan was rejected in Virginia as it was in other colonies.[18]

In November, Dunmore declared martial law and promised freedom to all blacks who took up the Royal cause. He followed up his proclamation with an offensive action using British troops under Colonel Leslie. At Great Bridge (near Norfolk) on January 1, 1776, the Redcoats were defeated by the militia under William

Woodford. Dunmore then turned his guns on Norfolk and "with some connivance from the Patriots" the town was destroyed.[19]

The County Committee of Fincastle was among the first to send troops to Williamsburg to assist the local militia. Captain William Campbell commanded a company of "choice riflemen" from Fincastle. This company served under Colonel Woodford, taking part in the first engagement of the war in Virginia in which blood was shed.[20] Fincastle had earlier sent Dunmore a letter expressing its gratitude to him for the service he had rendered the frontier in the expedition against the Indians.[21] The actions of Dunmore in removing the powder, however, quickly changed Fincastle's opinion of him. On July 10, 1775, the County Committee agreed that the governor's conduct reflected much dishonor on him and he justly deserved the censure universally bestowed. The committee then resolved that the actions of Patrick Henry and others who had opposed Dunmore justly merited the committee's hearty approbation and thanks. It further resolved "that we will, at the risk of our lives and fortunes, support and justify them with regard to the reprisal they made."[22]

Since the General Assembly of Virginia could no longer function, it was necessary to provide a new form of government, and under the direction of the Committee of Safety the historic Fifth Virginia Convention assembled on May 6, 1776. It was at this convention, too, that the Virginia delegates to the Second Continental Congress were instructed to support American independence. For such a tremendously important occasion, the people of Fincastle chose Colonel Arthur Campbell, as he was now known, and William Russell to represent them. Campbell's election is an indication of his popularity in Southwest Virginia at the time, and it reveals the high esteem in which he was held by the people.

According to a close observer, Campbell's "gallant services [at the Convention of 1776] deserve a deliberate record," for he exercised "a commanding position."[23] Campbell served on a variety of committees at the convention, and although he was not a public speaker, his influence was great.[24] On the second day of the session, he was appointed to serve on a committee with Patrick Henry, Archibald Cary, Henry Lee, and other distinguished men, who were instructed to prepare an ordinance for the encouragement of making salt, saltpeter, and gunpowder.[25] Campbell was greatly influenced by Patrick Henry, whom he considered his teacher on matters concerning the Revolution, and although years later political differences developed between them, Campbell always admired Henry.[26] On May 20, he was added to the Committee of Propositions and Grievances.[27]

It was commonly recognized that Campbell was the best informed man at Williamsburg on matters related to Indian affairs.[28] When the convention was informed that some Indians on the Ohio River were angry over the encroachment of their lands, he was appointed to a committee to investigate the problem.[29] Campbell was also appointed to a committee to collect evidence on behalf of the government against several people, primarily Richard Henderson, who claimed lands within the boundary of Virginia under deeds and purchases from the Indians. Campbell probably should not have served on this committee, for he was interested in acquiring land under Henderson's questionable claim. Even Patrick Henry, soon to be governor of Virginia, had an interst in Henderson's project.[30]

Petitions were pouring in from county after county urging the Convention to call for independence from Great Britain.[31] On May 15, the Convention resolved itself into a committee on the state of the colony to examine the issue. After some time in discussion it was unanimously agreed by the 112 members present to instruct the Virginia delegates appointed to the Continental Congress "to declare the United Colonies free and independent states, absolved from all allegiance to or dependent upon the Crown or Parliament of Great Britain."[32] By May 27, the resolutions calling for independence had been transmitted to the Virginia delegates in Congress. They "lay on the table of Congress like a bomb with a sputtering fuse, [and] not long could they be ignored...," wrote Edmond Cody Burnett.[33] They were not ignored for long. On June 7, Richard Henry Lee presented the resolutions to the Congress and on July 2, Congress voted that "these united colonies are and of right ought to be free and independent...."[34]

John Adams wrote to his wife Abigail on the same day:

> The Second day of July, 1776, will be the most memorable epoch in the history of America, I am apt to believe that it will be

celebrated by succeeding generations as the great anniversary festival. It ought to be commemorated, as the day of deliverance, by solemn acts of devotion to God Almighty. It ought to be solemnized with pomp and parade, with shows, games, sports, guns, bells, bonfires, and illuminations, from one end of this continent to the other, from this time forward, forevermore.[35]

And so it has been celebrated, but on July 4, the day Congress approved the Declaration of Independence, which explained to the world, including reluctant Americans, why it was necessary to take such a step.

After instructing its delegates to Congress to call for independence, the Virginia Convention adopted a resolution to appoint a committee to frame a declaration of rights and a plan of government for the state. A committee of over 30 members was given the task of framing a Declaration of Rights which became a model for other colonies in creating bills of rights. The Declaration was submitted to the House on May 27 and discussed until June 12 when it was unanimously adopted.[36] The records do not indicate what part Campbell played in the framing of the Declaration of Rights, but according to Henry Howe he was strongly opposed to an established church.[37] Although the Convention did not disestablish the Church it did take a step forward in the direction of religious freedom. Paragraph 18 of the Declaration declared that

religion, or the duty which we owe to our Creator, and the manner of discharging it, can be directed only be reason and conviction, not by force or violence; and therefore all men are equally entitled to the free exercise of religion, according to the dictates of conscience; and that it is the mutual duty of all to practice Christian forbearance, love, and charity toward each other.[38]

A constitution was submitted on June 26 and after three days of debate it was unanimously adopted. The Covention then turned its attention toward the election of a governor, council of state, and an attorney general. Patrick Henry was elected governor, with 60 votes to 45 of his closest rival, Thomas Nelson. A common seal was approved and provisions were made for publishing and distributing the new Constitution throughout the colony. The Convention adjourned on the day after the Continental Congress declared the American Colonies independent of Great Britain.[39]

While Campbell was at Williamsburg the dreaded war with the Cherokees broke out. The successful conclusion of Dunmore's War increased land hunting activities along the Ohio River, the Watauga and Holston Valleys, and beyond Cumberland Gap. John Stuart, British superintendent of Indian affairs in the South, reported in 1776 that hundreds of families had settled on the Watauga and Holston rivers beyond boundary lines agreed upon in treaties with the Indians. Extensive and populous settlements had also been established in Kentucky, where Richard Henderson made his Transylvania purchase the year before.[40] Chincanacina, "the Dragging Canoe," one of the most bitter foes of the whites, complained bitterly to Henry Stuart, deputy superintendent: "the white men have almost surrounded us leaving us only a little spot of ground to stand upon, and it seems to be their intention to destroy us as a nation."[41] The Cherokee Nation encompassed all the territory in the northwestern part of Georgia, western North and South Carolina, and Southwest Virginia. The Cherokees were the most warlike of the southern tribes and were familiar with the white man's weapons and military tactics. The Cherokee country was divided into three areas, the Lower Towns, the Middle Settlements and Valleys, and the Overhill Towns.[42] For good reason the Cherokees feared the loss of their land. Urged on by the young warriors, notably Dragging Canoe, they commenced hostilities. At first small bands of braves attacked isolated families, but a well organized, full scale Indian war was in the making.

During the summer of 1776, the Fincastle County Committee was busy organizing the militia in anticipation of war with Great Britain and the Cherokee Nation. Campbell was busy too, impressing upon the Virginia Convention the necessity of its aid in preparing the frontier counties for war. On May 28, he wrote the Fincastle Committee that he hoped he could soon send an order for raising an additional force for the frontier and that "700 wt. powder" and "2,000 gun flints" were being sent. Arrangements for additional supplies had also been made.[43] On June 10, Campbell's hoped for ordinance was passed by the Convention. Six companies of militia were to be called to duty as ranger companies in Fincastle.[44]

The assistance that Campbell was able to get from the Virginia Convention might not have been adequate had the frontier not been warned by an Indian woman named Nancy Ward of an independent attack. Nancy Ward lived at the Overhill town of Great Echota. Her father was a white man, her mother, the sister of chief Allakullaculla, "the Little Carpenter." Known as "Beloved Woman," she exercised great influence over the Cherokees, and even had the authority to spare the lives of prisoners captured in raids on frontier settlements. She was a friend of the whites and had it not been for this friendship, John Sevier at Watauga would not have known of the impending attack on the frontier settlements in July, 1776. The Indians planned to strike the frontiers of Virginia, the Carolinas, and Georgia simultaneously. The Overhill warriors, numbering about 700, were to attack Virginia. The Holston settlements were to be attacked by 300 warriors under Dragging Canoe. Old Abraham of Chilhowie was to attack Watauga, and the Raven planned to strike Carter's Valley. When Sevier learned of this he immediately wrote to the officers of Fincastle County that 600 Indians and Loyalists were about to start for Fort Lee with the intention of pushing on up the country to New River.[45]

Preparation for defense was made and five companies of militia, consisting of about 170 men, met at Eaton's Station, five miles below the junction of the two forks of the Holston. On July 20 the troops marched a few miles below the fort to Long Island Flats. Here they met an equal number of Indians led by Dragging Canoe. Firing commenced and Dragging Canoe was one of the first hit. With a bullet through both thighs he was taken to the rear of the Indian line, all the while exhorting his warriors to carry on the fight. However, the Cherokees soon retreated leaving 13 of their men dead. After the lesson learned at the Battle of Long Island Flats, Dragging Canoe never again attempted an all out battle with the militia. Hereafter, he used the familiar tactics of hit and run, making it practically impossible to predict the place of attack.[46]

On the same day of the Battle of Long Island Flats, Old Abraham was repulsed at Watauga by John Carter, James Robertson, John Sevier and a small group of men, some of whom had fought side by side with the Virginians at the Battle of Point Pleasant two years before. The westernmost settlement at Carter's Valley was evacuated and the Raven met little resistance. The Indians burned cabins, killed livestock, and then broke up into small parties, striking on the Clinch River. One party struck at Wolf Hills, a short distance from the home of Campbell's cousin, William.[47]

William Campbell, expressing the attitude of the inhabitants on the frontier, wrote Arthur Campbell early in August, 1776, "I am under the most dreadful apprehension for the people of [the Holston] from the barbarous disposition of the enemy," partly the results of British influence.[48] It was decided to take the war into the Indian country and a coordinated invasion consisting of militia from Virginia, the Carolinas and Georgia took place. Colonel William Christian, the commander of the Virginia troops, was ordered by the Virginia Council to severely chastise "that cruel and perfidious nation . . . in a manner most likely to put a stop to future insults and ravages." With the mistaken belief that the British had instigated the conflict, the Council further ordered Christian to bring back with him those responsible for bringing on the war, "particularly Stuart, Cameron and Gist, and all others who have committed murders or robberies on our frontier."[49]

On October 1, 1776, Christian left Long Island on the Holston for the Indian towns. Meeting little opposition, within 20 days he had taken control of all but the deserted towns. At Christian's discretion some of the towns were burned and the chiefs were compelled to talk peace, but Dragging Canoe failed to appear. Instead of talking peace, he took his war party down to Chickamauga and for the next four years continued to raid the frontier settlements.[50] Nevertheless, a formal treaty was concluded at Fort Henry on the Holston, July 20, 1777. Known as the Treaty of Long Island, a line was agreed to which ran from Cumberland Gap to the junction of Cloud's Creek and the Holston, then to Chimney Top Mountain, to Camp Creek on the south bank of the Nolichucky and southwest to the Georgia line. A month before, treaties were signed between the Cherokees and the states of South Carolina and Georgia. These combined treaties resulted in the Indians' ceding millions of acres of land.[51] The treaties also brought a few years of relative calm in the south, freeing the frontiersman to concentrate once again on the northern tribes who, with British support, were threatening the Kentucky settlements.

4 Father of Washington County

Although independence was the primary concern of the American people in 1776, other significant events were taking place. Elections were held in Fincastle County late in the summer for members of the House of Delegates. Satisfied with the performances of Campbell and Russell at the Virginia Convention, the people of Fincastle sent them back to the Legislature in the fall of the year. Campbell, now 33 years old, had already earned a high reputation as a patriot and a military officer. His political agility was about to come to light. However, he lost his first important political contest in the Virginia Assembly when he opposed George Rogers Clark and Thomas Jefferson, who wanted to make Kentucky a separate county. Because of his obstinacy over this issue, Campbell made a number of enemies ealry in his political career and many of his contemporaries would have agreed with Clark's biographer, who described Campbell as "an ambitious and unlovable Scot . . . , a chronic malcontent and a disturber of the peace along the frontiers."[1]

Kentucky, with all its beauty and potential for profit was the land speculators' dream. Of all those who competed for Kentucky, it was Richard Henderson of North Carolina and his associates who dominated. Henderson, a North Carolina Superior Court judge, sent Daniel Boone to Kentucky in 1769 to locate the best lands. When the judge retired from public life in 1773, he and a few other North Carolina men interested in land projects established the

39

Louisa Company. Two years later the company reorganized and
the name was changed to the Transylvania Company. A meeting
was held at Sycamore Shoals in March, 1775, between Henderson,
with several hundred white men, and some twelve hundred Indians, including Oconostota, Attakullaculla and Dragging Canoe,
the purpose of which was to obtain millions of acres of land from
the Cherokees. For the price of about "ten thousand British pounds
of sterling, in money and in goods," the Indians ceded a tract of land
which consisted of most of the future state of Kentucky and much
of Tennessee. Supposedly, Dragging Canoe, objecting to the sale,
rose up and pointing toward Kentucky, warned that a dark cloud
hung over that "bloody ground."[2] By this time Daniel Boone had
already extended the Wilderness Road into Kentucky and established Boonesborough. Henderson, however, had not moved fast
enough, for there were settlers already in Kentucky, particularly at
a place called Harrodsburg, and these pioneers would never recog-
nize Henderson's claim to Kentucky.

The "Lord Proprietors" followed up their deal with the Indians
by establishing an independent colony called Transylvania. On the
surface, the government of Transylvania appeared to be relatively
democratic, but in actuality, it contained many of the feudal trap-
pings that John Locke proposed in his Fundamental Constitution
for the Carolinas in 1669, and like Carolinians, who rejected
Locke's plan, many inhabitants of Kentucky would never support
Henderson's government. This became all the more obvious as the
people back east moved closer toward the Revolution.

Henderson had other problems too. Both the royal governors
of Virginia and North Carolina objected to the land purchased at
Sycamore Shoals, for Transylvania lay within both colonies, most
of which was a part of western Fincastle County, Virginia. The
legality of individuals or companies purchasing land from the Indians was also questioned.[3]

Nevertheless, in defiance of the royal governors of Virginia and
North Carolina, Henderson proceeded to organize what amounted
to an independent state. Virginia officials were alarmed. William
Preston wrote George Washington that the Kentucky situation
"will soon become a serious affair and highly deserves the attention
of the government." Once a large number of settlers go out there,

he wrote, it "will be next to impossible to remove them or reduce them to obedience."[4] Many prominent men including Preston, Washington, and Patrick Henry were opposed to Henderson's ownership of Kentucky, for they had plans of their own in Kentucky. Among those who had already acquired large tracts there, or who were seeking land, were Arthur Campbell, William Byrd, George Washington, Andrew Lewis, William Preston, William Christian, and Patrick Henry.[5]

Arthur Campbell had more than a passing interest in the fate of Henderson's company, but whereas many of the leading Virginians were opposed to Henderson, Campbell supported him. Campbell had accompanied Henderson part of the way into Kentucky and there is reason to believe he acquired land in Transylvania under Henderson's title, for he was in Boonesborough in December, 1775, staking out a claim. Campbell also wanted to be a surveyor for the colony. It was, therefore, in Campbell's interest that Henderson's colony succeed.[6]

While Campbell was in Transylvania he was almost killed by Indians. Unarmed, he and two young lads named Saunders and McQuinney crossed the Kentucky River. Once across the river they parted company, the boys going up a nearby hill and Campbell going up the river. About ten minutes later the inhabitants of the stockade heard a gun shot and a cry of distress. Someone shouted that Campbell had been shot. A rescue party rushed out and saw Campbell fleeing to the landing after being shot at by a couple of Indians. In his haste he had lost one of his shoes. Daniel Boone immediately led out a search party, but it was days before they found McQuinney, who had been scalped; Saunders was never found.[7]

In addition to his interest in Transylvania, Campbell had also been taking up land from the Loyal Company. He had 293 acres in Fincastle County on the north side of the Clinch River, recorded May 20, 1774. The next year 1215 acres lying on both sides of the Middle Fork of the Holston, 701 acres of which were from the Loyal Company, were recorded for him.[8] In addition to these tracts, a thousand acres lying at the Falls of the Ohio were recorded for him in June, 1774, under a warrant from Governor Dunmore. This latter survey was for his services in the French and Indian War.[9]

Other well known men were involved in similar activities. In the summer of 1774, both Patrick Henry and William Christian wrote Campbell that they wanted to buy some land from the Cherokees. In order to facilitate the purchase, Henry sent William Kennedy to Campbell with the hope that Campbell would assist Kennedy on his mission to the Cherokees to determine if they were willing to sell some land. Henry informed Campbell that he and "some other gentlemen" were going to form a partnership in order to make a "snug little purchase" from the Cherokees. A similar letter from Christian went into more detail concerning the partnership, naming the "other gentlemen" who turned out to be William Byrd, John Page, Ralph Wormeley, Samuel Overton and a number of others. Christian seemed to want to make a small purchase at first and if this worked out, a large purchase could be made at a later time. After his trip to the Cherokee towns, Kennedy informed Campbell that the Indians were in need of goods, and he believed they would sell if goods were available at the time of the negotiations.[10]

Henderson now moved quickly to make his own Transylvania purchase, but he did not wish to alienate such an important man as Henry. He asked Campbell if he thought Henry would be interested in becoming a partner. Campbell informed him that Henry had indicated that he would like to. Later, however, when all this came to public attention, Campbell, apparently wanting to protect Henry from public censure, minimized Henry's interest, stating that because of his own concern for the success of the company he may have overstated the case concerning Henry's wish to become a partner.[11]

When publicly questioned about his land speculating activities, Henry admitted that he had looked into the possibility of purchasing Indian lands and that Henderson had asked him to become a partner, but the conflict with Great Britain ended his interest. He was offered shares in a number of land projects, Henry pointed out, but refused them because of the controversy that had arisen and because he thought it improper for a man in his position (now governor of Virginia) to become a party in such projects. He also stated that he believed all Indian country would probably come under state authority.[12] Henry was right, for the states, or the Confederation Congress, did claim the land and the position he took was politically expedient. Even so, it was commonly understood among those in the know, that Henry and even Thomas Jefferson had, at one time or another, expressed an interest in Henderson's Company.[13] When the Revolution got underway however, and the land in question came under the control of the Virginia Assembly, many of those who supported or seemed to support Henderson, changed their minds. Jefferson, for example, wanted to see the west opened up to individual farmers possessing a minimum of 50 acres, thus, he would become the land speculators' worst enemy. Patrick Henry, too would later speak out against Henderson.[14] Henderson, in the meantime, made a futile effort to gain the support of the Virginia Assembly and the Continental Congress. The Continental Congress refused to support him until Virginia did, and Virginia's support Henderson would never get.

The people living in Transylvania under the government established by Henderson soon became dissatisfied. This dissatisfaction was brought to the attention of the Virginia Convention in the form of a petition signed by 89 inhabitants. The petitioners stated that they had been lured by promises of easy terms to take up lands and settle in Transylvania, believing they would receive a valid title to their land. The company, in the meantime, had raised the purchase price and the surveying and entering fee. The inhabitants were also concerned that their lands lay beyond the boundary line established by the Treaty of Fort Stanwix. The petitioners implored the convention to take them under the protection of the state and to intervene in their behalf that they might not suffer under the demands and impositions of the "gentlemen styling themselves proprietors."[15]

On May 20, two petitions from the inhabitants of Pendleton District in the western part of Fincastle County, together with the proceedings of the County Committee of Fincastle were presented to the Convention. The petition complained that John Carter and Robert Lucas, in the neighboring settlement called Washington District, pretended to have purchased the petitioner's lands, and that the two men had seized the inhabitants' possessions without payment. Carter and Lucas gave notice to others who refused to pay exorbitant prices for titles that they would be forced off the property. The petitioners requested that they be brought under the protection of Virginia. Numerous complaints such as these induced the Virginia Convention to create a committee for the purpose of collecting evidence on behalf of the government against those claiming to own lands under deeds purchased from the Indians. Campbell was appointed to this committee and it was at the hearings of this committee that the land projects of Henry and Henderson were publicly scrutinized.[16]

The inhabitants of Transylvania took matters into their own hands in June, 1776. Meeting at Harrodsburg they chose George Rogers Clark and Gabriel John Jones to take their case to the Virginia Assembly. According to the historian Archibald Henderson, the leader of the group of dissidents was George Rogers Clark.[17] Actually, the West's greatest defender against the land speculators was Thomas Jefferson, who championed the frontier inhabitants' cause in the General Assembly. Clark arrived at Williamsburg too late to go before the Assembly, because it had already adjourned, but he was able to see Governor Henry. Obviously enjoying Clark's denunciation of the Transylvania Company, Henry suggested that Clark take the matter before the Council of State. When Clark went before the Council of State he described the condition of the inhabitants of Kentucky, emphasizing their vulnerability to Indian attacks. Virginia must do something, he asserted, otherwise the Kentucky settlements would come under the control of the English and their Indian allies. When the council agreed to provide the necessary ammunition for the Kentuckians to defend themselves, Clark knew that it would only be a matter of time before Virginia extended total authority over Kentucky, and Transylvania would cease to exist.[18]

It was not until the autumn of 1776 that Clark was able to bring the Kentucky issue before the Assembly. The land companies also sought the Assembly's support, with Henderson challenging Virginia's right to claim the territory he had purchased. Yet early in the session it appeared that Henderson's Transylvania was doomed. On October 11 the representatives from western Fincastle were denied seats in the Assembly, but at the same time the House Committee of the Whole resolved that the inhabitants should be formed into a distinct county.[19]

The most outspoken opponent of Clark's plan to make

Kentucky a separate county was Campbell. He publicly advocated that Kentucky remain a part of Fincastle, for he realized that a new county would deprive him of influence over a vast region which had held out so many possibilities to him.[20] Campbell's connection with Henderson's Company has already been noted and it appears that he would have much to gain if Henderson's purchase was ruled legal.

Campbell's case soon appeared hopeless. The bill for dividing Fincastle into two distinct counties received a second reading and was given to a committee, of which Thomas Jefferson and the delegates from Augusta and Botetourt counties were members. On October 24, after two readings, the committee to which the bill was referred was discharged and the next day a third reading was denied.[21] Campbell, whom a contemporary described as "very able, mean-spirited and jealous," continued to use every means he could to defeat the measure.[22]

It was at this stage, according to Clark's biographer, that an enmity developed between Campbell and Clark that was to last for years.[23] With the defeat of the bill seemingly certain, Clark and Jones were about to give up the fight and return to Kentucky, but after a week of setback after setback, the bill secured another first reading. It was read a second time and presented to a committee headed by Jefferson and including Campbell. The committee was ordered to receive a clause or clauses for forming Kentucky into a distinct county. George Mason, another friend of the bill was added to the committee. Campbell could not prevent the committee from agreeing on the bill, and on November 23, it was ordered to be engrossed and read a third time after which it was passed by the House.[24]

Campbell took the bill, as passed by the House, to the Senate. The Senate refused to approve it and a deadlock ensued. For 15 days the bill was debated, with messages passing between the two houses. Each house refused to yield. Finally, on December 7, 1776, the Senate withdrew its objections and the bill creating Kentucky County became a law. The bill divided Fincastle into three distinct counties, instead of the previous plan of two counties—Kentucky, Washington and Montgomery.[25] Fincastle was lost in the division and Campbell's Royal Oak now lay in Washington County, which also included much of the future counties of Russell, Scot, Smyth, Tazewell, Lee, Buchanan, Dickenson, and Wise.

Jefferson, who served on the Propositions and Grievances Committee with Campbell, was responsible more than anyone else in the Assembly for the bill making Kentucky a separate county. However he did more than that, according to Julian P. Boyd, for the bill

> not only asserted the sovereignty of Virginia over the Kentucky region claimed by Transylvania, but it dealt another blow to the conservative Tidewater dominance over political affairs within the state. Arrayed against him in this struggle were the most powerful forces in Virginia – the plantation aristocracy of the East and their allies, the land capitalists, who sought to exploit the West for profit. Against this powerful combination he had won a signal victory.[26]

Ironically, it was not all defeat for Campbell, as he was appointed to the top militia position of county lieutenant for Washington County. He was also commissioned a justice of the peace in the new county and became presiding justice of the Washington County Court.[27] Thus, his status as a public figure was raised considerably as a result of the passage of the Kentucky bill he had opposed so vigorously.

The act establishing Washington County provided for the creation of a county court which was to meet at Black's Fort on the last Tuesday in January, 1777. The members of the court, commissioned by the governor, were men who had already distinguished themselves in Southwest Virginia, and included Arthur Campbell, John Campbell, William Campbell, Joseph Martin, Evan Shelby and Daniel Smith.[28]

The first Washington County Court convened on January 28, 1777. Campbell was the first justice named and was the first to be sworn into office. After taking the oath of office he administered the oath to the others. James Dysart took the oath of sheriff and Arthur's brother, David, was appointed clerk of the court. After the sheriff opened the court, Campbell, who had been commissioned county lieutenant by the Virginia Committee of Safety, took the oath for that position.[29]

The responsibilities of the county lieutenant were many as he was the highest ranking militia officer in the county. In case of impending war it was his responsibility to call a council of war consisting of his field officers and captains. The captains were usually required to provide a list of all the eligible draftees for the militia. On one occasion in March, 1777, for example, he wrote James Robertson, a captain in the militia of Washington County, but living at Watauga, to furnish him with a list of the settlers at Watauga. He needed the list, Campbell pointed out, in order to know the strength of the community and to give necessary orders for the inhabitants' protection.[30]

It was the county lieutenant's ultimate responsibility to see that a sufficient number of militia men were called into action in the event of an enemy threat, and he acted as coordinator of the companies, seeing to the proper utilization of men and resources. He also had the extremely difficult task of seeing that his men were properly paid for their service to the county. This was one of Campbell's biggest headaches and he was constantly writing the governor for funds to pay his men. The county lieutenant kept in close contact with the same official in other counties, and with the governor; this resulted in a high degree of efficiency when officers of the various county militia carried out their orders, although this was often not the case. When the county lieutenant accompanied his men on campaigns, he ranked as colonel, the colonels ranked as lieutenants colonels, and the lieutenant colonels as majors.[31]

Because of his position, the county lieutenant could become a significant statewide political figure, as he came in contact with many of the important men of the state from the governor on down. It often happened that the person holding this office also occupied other important offices in the county. This was true of Campbell, who from time to time held, in addition to his military office, the position of presiding judge of the county court, justice of the peace, sheriff, surveyor and delegate to the General Assembly.

Campbell was the presiding judge of the Washington County Court for 33 years, retiring in 1800. Justices were known for their irregular attendance in court and Campbell, living 30 miles from the courthouse and involved in frontier defense, did not attend very regularly. When he did take his seat on the bench there was uncommon deference paid him, both by members of the court and the lawyers present. He presided with great dignity and earned a high reputation for his knowledge of the law.[32]

In the spring of 1777, Campbell ran for a second term in the Virginia Assembly. To qualify to vote, every free white man must have had 20 acres of land with a house and plantation on it for at least a year, or if no house and plantation, then 100 acres were required. He might also vote if he had a right to his wife's estate if her estate met the required stipulations,[33] but of course, his wife could not vote. In this election, Campbell and William Edmiston ran against William Cocke and Anthony Bledsoe. After an especially vigorous campaign, Campbell and his running mate lost the election. They immediately filed a complaint against the election returns with the House of Delegates. In the complaint they argued that although Cocke and Bledsoe obtained the highest number of votes, they did so because many of the votes were cast by persons living in North Carolina and by other persons who did not possess the qualifications for voting. Campbell and Edmiston also argued that Bledsoe should be disqualified from sitting in the Legislature because of his military command and that Cocke did not possess the required property in the county. They also claimed that there were cases of bribery and corruption during the election.[34]

The Committee on Privileges and Elections examined the charges. Concerning the legality of the votes, the Committee accepted the returns submitted by the sheriff of Washington County: Bledsoe, 297; Cocke, 294; Campbell, 211; and Edmiston, 144. The finding on the second charge, concerning Bledsoe's military rank, also went against the petitioners, the Committee pointing out that he held no other rank than major in the militia. As to the third charge, the Committee found that Cocke did have sufficient land in Washington County to qualify him to run, and they found the charge of bribery and corruption groundless. The Committee concluded that Cocke and Bledsoe were duly elected to serve as delegates in the General Assembly.[35] It was Campbell's conduct in affairs such as this that caused his nephew to write many years later: Campbell's disposition required that he "have his own way and with the greatest obstinacy to persevere in carrying out what he undertook."[36]

Although Campbell appears to have used the argument purely for his own selfish purposes, later developments showed that he was right about the boundary line between North Carolina and Virginia. It becomes all the more interesting when William Cocke himself later argued that the area in dispute during the election of 1777 was in North Carolina. On October 20, 1779, a year after Cocke had served in the General Assembly, a complaint was filed that he interfered with the deputy sheriff while he was performing the duties of tax collector on the north side of the Holston River in Carter's Valley. Cocke had urged the people not to pay taxes to Virginia since they lived in North Carolina. One can imagine the feelings of Arthur Campbell at this time as he was not only a justice on the court, but also the sheriff and he was now in a position to deal with one of his chief antagonists on his own terms. The court ordered that Cocke's conduct be reported to the governor.[37] The outcome, however, was not what Campbell expected for an investigation over the affair resulted in a reduction of the territory included in Washington County.

The Virginia Assembly and the General Assembly of North Carolina appointed commissioners to run the boundary line between the two states. The commissioners ran the line about 40 miles, at which point they could not agree. The Virginia commissioners, Thomas Walker and William B. Smith, proceeded to run the line to the Mississippi resulting in a reduction of about a third to a half of the territory then comprising Washington County. This line was immediately accepted by the Virginia Assembly and later the North Carolina General Assembly.[38]

While Washington County was in the process of being reduced in size, Arthur Campbell and others were attempting to increase its growth another way—through the establishment of a new town to be called Abingdon. On April 29, 1777, the county appointed Campbell and six others as trustees to utilize the 120 acres of land given to the county by Thomas Walker, Joseph Black and Samuel Briggs.[39] The trustees then instructed John Coulter to survey and lay out the main street of the town of Abingdon. This done, the trustees began to sell lots, but found it difficult to dispose of the lots because of some uncertainty in the title to the property. Campbell and ten other members of the county court sent a petition to the

House of Delegates in the fall of 1777. They pointed out that the land was acquired from Walker, Black and Briggs and the other men, for the purpose of erecting a town and

> Whereas it is apprehended that it would much conduce to the speedy settlement of the aforesaid town and advance the value of the lots if an act of [the] Assembly should pass, enabling the said court or their trustees to receive titles from the above named gentlemen for the land given and sold, and also to enable them to lay off, sell and make conveyances to the purchasers, and grant such privileges and immunities to the settlers on such lots, as to citizens in like cases have been granted, in the premises we submit to the consideration of your honorable House, and pray you to grant us such redress as you judge just and right....[40]

The petition was referred to a committee on November 8, 1777, but was not heard again until Campbell returned to the House of Delegates in the fall of 1778. Neither Cocke nor Bledsoe showed any particular interest in the matter during their term in the Assembly, but as a result of Campbell's efforts, the town of Abingdon was incorporated on October 3, 1778.[41] Along with this accomplishment on behalf of the people of Abingdon, as Summers has noted, Campbell "played such an important part in the history of Washington County as would justly entitle him to the appellation of 'Father of Washington County' so intelligent and active were his efforts in the settling of ... [the] county and in the protection of its earlier habitants...."[42]

5 Revolution in the West

When Americans declared their indepedence in July, 1776, they realized that in order to actually obtain it, they would have to fight a war against the most powerful country in the world. But even the British army was not adequate for the task of subduing the rebellious colonists. This became even more the case after the battle of Saratoga, New York, in October, 1777, and the military alliance between the United States and France the following year. Consequently, to supplement its own pool of men, the British government recruited some 15,000 Scots and 30,000 highly trained German soldiers to fight the Americans. Thousands of Loyalists and Indian allies made the enemy even more formidable.

The Americans, on the other hand, always suffered from a shortage of men. George Washington, commander in chief of the Continental Army, frequently pleaded with the Congress for additional men. The request was passed on down to the state governors who in turn begged the county lieutenants for county militia. Seldom did Washington get the men he needed, and even if he did, desertions created still another problem. Little wonder that just five months after independencee was declared, Thomas Paine found it necessary to write that "these are the times that try men's souls. The summer soldier and the sunshine patriot will, in this crisis, shrink from the service of his country, but he that stands now deserves the love and thanks of man and woman...."[1]

Washington rarely had over 18,000 men under his immediate command so he used "hit and run" tactics during most of the conflict, causing British officers to complain that Washington would not stand and fight. With such a one-sided situation, Washington knew not to "stand and fight" for had he done so, it is probable that the war would have ended quite differently. With rare exception, the British never adjusted to the American way of fighting, and in the end they lost. Before they lost, however, the British continued the war for six years.[2]

No part of the country was exposed to more constant or greater danger during the Revolution than the settlements in Southwest Virginia and Kentucky. The threat of war with the Northern tribes was even greater after the British became their ally. On the Southern frontier there was a constant dread of the Cherokees and Chicamaugas, and danger from Loyalist activity. The manner in which these dangers were faced had a profound effect on the outcome of the American Revolution, and Arthur Campbell, although often in the background, played an important part in these events.

When commissioned county lieutenant of Washington County in January, 1777, Campbell took command of the newly organized county militia, the 70th Regiment. Other high ranking officers of the regiment included Colonel Evan Shelby, Lieutenant Colonel William Campbell, and Major Daniel Smith. Among the other officers were captains William Edmiston, Joseph Martin, Robert Craig, and James Robertson, the latter of whom resided at Watauga.[3] One of Campbell's most difficult problems as commander was preventing friction among the men in his county, who were always fearful that one might rise above the other in power and prominence. The case of Anthony Bledsoe is illustrative. When the regiment was formed Bledsoe failed to get a militia commission because Campbell advised the governor that Bledsoe had settled or was going to settle in Kentucky County. Bledsoe filed a complaint with the Virginia Council, but the Council found Campbell's position justified and Bledsoe was denied a commission. A similar complaint was filed by James Thompson who also failed to receive a commission, but the Council again supported Campbell.[4]

According to tradition, the two leading antagonists were Arthur Campbell and his cousin William Campbell. It has been said that these two extremely proud and independent men were jealous of one another. In order to keep peace in the family, therefore, they agreed to alternate command of expeditions against the enemy.[5] While there may have been such an agreement, their correspondence suggests that rather than being jealous of one another they were close comrades. However, if there was rivalry between them it was not confined to the Campbells alone, for Evan Shelby did not trust John Sevier, while Sevier and Isaac Shelby were jealous of William Campbell.[6] Rivalry was not uncommon on the frontier, or for that matter among practically any group of proud and independent men. But when a crisis occurred, such petty feelings were usually overcome and all worked together to oppose the enemy.

The Treaty of Long Island in 1777 kept the Cherokees quiet for a while, but the Northwestern tribes, under British influence were restless. Reports of scattered attacks along the frontier throughout August, 1777, were reported to General Edward Hand, commander of Fort Pitt. Campbell wrote William Fleming of an attack on two men, 50 miles down Sandy River. The men escaped and warned the inhabitants in the area, although one settler was killed and scalped on the Clinch River. Under this threat the people on the Clinch rushed to the fort which had been built, but they continued to be in utmost distressing circumstances. The need for men, provisions, salt and lead were great. Despairingly, Campbell asked, "Can no plan be made to chastise these savages? Can nothing be done at Fort Pitt?"[7]

The treacherous murder of the Shawnee chief, Cornstalk, in the autumn of the year, compounded the danger on the Virginia frontier. He had gone to a fort at the mouth of Kanawha to warn the whites that the Shawnee were about to join the British. Once inside the fort Cornstalk was killed by soldiers who were angry because one of their own men had just been killed by Indians.[8] "The late barbarous, inhuman and impolitic murder committed at the Point on the Cornstalk and his party," wrote Preston, "will be followed by the most direful consequences to this long extended frontier." He did not believe that such a "warlike, blood-thirsty and revengeful nation" as the Shawnee would let the murder of their leader pass without revenge. It was more likely, he thought, that with the assistance of the British at Detroit, a new confederacy of northern tribes would be formed and a desperate attack would soon be made on the frontier from Pittsburgh to the lower settlements of the Clinch and Kentucky rivers.[9] Preston's predictions proved all too true.

By the spring of 1778, Indian raids around Fort Pitt became so frequent that it was doubtful the American position there could be held. Virginia was the first to suffer from the Northwest Indians. In May, a force of Wyandottes and Mingoes attacked Fort Randolph. According to Campbell, this party consisted of some 200 or 300 warriors. In the attack on the fort, a James Gilmore was wounded and the cattle were killed or carried off. The next day the men in the fort talked to the Indians about a peace treaty, which the Indians agreed to consider, but they marched toward the interior settlements instead. A messenger sent from Fort Randolph was able to warn the people on the Greenbriar in time, and the entire settlement of 25 men and 60 women and children reached their little fort in time.

The attack came at daybreak. All day long the defenders of the fort repulsed the red men. At four o'clock the whites were reinforced by Samuel Lewis and 70 others who fought their way through the Indians to the safety of the fort. The Indians finally decided it was useless to continue the fight and retreated, leaving 17 of their number dead. One white man in the garrison was killed and another wounded. Outside the fort the Indians killed two men and a boy.[10]

It was generally agreed that Detroit would have to be taken from the British before peace would come to the West. Fort Detroit was commanded by Colonel Henry Hamilton, known as the "hair buyer," because it was said that he offered rewards to Indians for Patriot scalps. Detroit, therefore, became the ultimate goal of the Patriots in the West. Commissioners from Virginia and Pennsylvania met in the spring of 1778, and agreed that an expedition ought to be organized to take Detroit. On June 11, the Continental Congress agreed to request that the governor and council of Virginia call up the militia in the event it became necessary to assist in the campaign against Detroit.

Meanwhile, Virginia was having a difficult time obtaining adequate supplies in order to defend its own borders. To supply men and equipment for an expedition against Detroit was out of the question. Describing the distressed condition on the Clinch River at this time, Major Daniel Smith wrote Campbell, June 19, "I am much pained at our situation here. There is not, I believe, more than 40 men on duty all telling me they are not to be got to leave their homes. They are very badly provided with provisions, part of what is used has been borrowed from the settlers in the forks, who have it not to spare."[11] A month later Campbell was pleading with William Campbell for "1,000 good flints." He had ordered some while at Williamsburg but had not yet received them. Campbell complained that his militia had only flint that could be found in the woods.[12] Washington County was, therefore, in no position to assist in an expedition against Detroit. Other frontier counties faced similar problems, thus the campaign had to be postponed.

The Continental Congress settled for an expedition against the Northwest tribes, and Virginia agreed. General Lachlan McIntosh, a Scotch Highlander who had emigrated to Georgia, was to lead the expedition. The Virginia Council advised the governor to direct the county lieutenants of Washington, Montgomery, Botetourt, Augusta, and other western counties to call up as many men as McIntosh might need.[13] Supplies and troops were gathered with such difficulty that the year 1778 ended without an expedition, while the British continued to supply the Indians for their attacks on the western settlements.

The new settlements in Kentucky were also in danger of being destroyed, as George Rogers Clark had warned two years before. Daniel Boone and 26 others were captured by a party of Indians near Blue Licks in February, 1778. Boone was eventually taken to the Indian town of Chillicothe where more than 400 warriors had gathered in preparation for an attack on Boonesborough. Boone escaped and warned the settlers. Arthur Campbell sent word of the dilemma to the governor and Council in August of 1778, and requested "the advice of the Council with respect to what had best be done in the matter...." The Council advised the governor to direct Campbell to send some men from his militia, "not under 100 nor exceeding, 150," to relieve the people of Kentucky.[14] A body of men could readily be raised for that purpose as this might enable the Kentuckians to destroy some of the nearby Indian towns and bring relief to Campbell's own borders.[15] Throughout the remainder of the war, Campbell frequently sent men and supplies to the struggling settlements in Kentucky. The fact that the major settlements there were never taken by the enemy can be attributed in large measure to Campbell's concern for the Kentuckians.

George Rogers Clark, who had so favorably impressed Governor Henry two years before, now received his blessings to carry the war to the enemy's own country in the Northwest. Clark captured Kaskaskia on July 4, 1778, then Cahokia and Fort Sackville at Vincinnes. Hamilton retook Fort Sackville but was forced to give it up along with himself on February 25, 1779.[16]

Hamilton and 26 prisoners set out under guard for Williamsburg on March 8. Clark warned the British officer that he and his men would be in danger when they passed the frontier, and the reception they received at the Falls of the Ohio gave Hamilton cause to remember Clark's warning. At Harrodsburg the British prisoners saw the horror of Indian warfare, much of which they had been responsible for. "These poor inhabitants are worthy of pity," Hamilton later remarked.[17]

The prisoners reached the Holston Valley May 1 and on May 6 stayed overnight at Campbell's home. Hamilton was treated well at Royal Oak, but his men became belligerent and threatened revenge because they did not think they received proper provisions. Considering the contempt in which they were held by the mountain men of the frontier, the prisoners were fortunate to be treated as well as they were and to be allowed to leave for Williamsburg the next day. Campbell later wrote Hamilton that his father had served Hamilton's grandfather as a steward and had saved the officer's father from drowning in the Boyne. Campbell expressed regret that Hamilton had contributed so much to the distress of the frontier.[18]

Hamilton's plans for a spring campaign was shattered, but back east in Georgia the British had taken Savannah and Augusta. This enabled the Cherokees and Chickamaugas to be supplied by the British, and Dragging Canoe was again determined to destroy the Holston settlements. To deter this, Campbell's second in command, Evan Shelby, was sent with a force of 350 volunteers and an additional 150 men under John Montgomery to invade the Indian towns in April, 1779. Shelby burned the town of Chicakamauga and ten villages nearby and destroyed 20,000 bushels of corn, probably stockpiled for Hamilton's anticipated spring campaign. Cattle, horses and peltries along with British supplies were carried off and sold at auction.[19] A period of temporary tranquillity followed giving the mountain men the opportunity to deal with the increasing problem of Loyalist activity, and enabled them to assist the Patriots in the East at one of the darkest periods of the Revolutionary War.

The Loyalists on the frontier did not generally consist of original settlers, but were recent immigrants from New York, Connecticut and other eastern regions. At first, the Loyalists were content to remain quiet and inactive, but after British victories in Georgia and South Carolina, they attempted to aid the Redcoats.[20] One of the main areas of Loyalist activity was in the vicinity of the valuable lead mines on the New River in Montgomery County, Virginia. As early in the war as January, 1778, William Preston complained to Governor Henry that over a hundred inhabitants refused to take the oath of allegiance and had been disarmed.[21] They continued to cause the Patriots concern and the next year the Loyalists around the Yadkin and New River felt strong enough to attempt to destroy Chiswell's Lead Mines. When Preston, county lieutenant of Montgomery, was unable to thwart them, he sent an urgent request to Campbell for aid. Campbell dispatched 150 men under the command of William Campbell.[22]

Both Arthur and William Campbell treated Loyalists very harshly. William was especially hated by Loyalists, who frequently threatend the life of this "bloody tyrant of Washington County...,"[23] and Theodore Roosevelt observed that Patriots of the Watauga and Holston regions equated Loyalists with common criminals, murderers, horse thieves and the like. Illustrating this fact, Roosevelt described an event that occurred one Sunday afternoon in Washington County.

> [William] Campbell was returning from church with his wife and some friends, carrying his baby on a pillow in front of his saddle, for they were mounted. Suddenly, a horseman crossed the road close in front of them, and was recognized by one of the party as a noted Tory. Upon being challenged, he rode off at full speed. Instantly, Campbell handed the baby to a Negro slave, stuck spur into his horse, and galloping after the fugitive, overtook and captured him. The other men of the party came up a minute later.

Several recognized the prisoner as a well-known Tory; he had on him letters to the British agents among the Cherokees, arranging for an Indian rising. The party of returning churchgoers were accustomed to the quick and summary justice of lynch-law. With stern gravity, they organized themselves into a court. The prisoner was adjudged guilty, and was given but a short shrift; for the horsemen hung him to a sycamore tree before they returned to the road where they had left their families.[24]

On another occasion, a number of Loyalists from Black Lick in Wythe County were captured and hanged by William. When 1,300 Loyalists were routed at Ramseur's Mill in North Carolina by that state's militia, Arthur moved up the New River where he captured some who had escaped. Going back down the river he sent out parties to scan the countryside with orders to "disarm, distress and terrify the settlements" that had been the most active in joining the British.[25] Such treatment of Loyalists by the Campbells and others led the Virginia Assembly to pass a law justifying these acts and prohibiting any legal action against the Washington County militia.[26]

In July, 1780, Loyalists were still trying to destroy the vital lead mines, and Campbell went to the mines to take charge of the defense. William Campbell was sent up the New River where 40 or 50 Loyalists had gathered in preparation for a move against the mines. When William arrived, the Loyalists disbursed, fleeing into the mountain laurel thickets. One was captured and immediately shot.[27]

The British followed up their victories in Georgia by taking Charleston in May of 1780, followed by still another victory at Camden when General Cornwallis defeated General Gates. The defeat at Camden practically destroyed the Continental Army in the South. What was left of it was given to the brilliant Nathanael Greene who, along with Francis Marion, Daniel Morgan and others, conducted a guerrilla war in North and South Carolina. From this point on, the colonial militia in the South and West played an increasingly important role in the war. The Loyalists, too, would become more active.[28]

Under orders from Cornwallis, two cavalry officers, Lieutenant Colonel Banastre Tarleton, "Bloody Tarleton," and Major Patrick

Ferguson, began organizing the Loyalists as they moved through South Carolina. Orders were sent to the British Indian agent to encourage the Indians to strike the settlements west of the mountains and destroy Chiswell's Lead Mines. Ferguson planned to move across North Carolina and later form a junction with Cornwallis, who with the main body of troops, was moving along the road by way of Salisbury. Both armies were then to invade Virginia.[29]

Ferguson began his operation by marching toward the North Carolina mountains. He soon met a small force of militia under Colonel Charles McDowell and routed them. McDowell and about 150 of his men escaped across the mountain to the Patriot stronghold of Watauga. Ferguson threatened to cross the mountains, hang the Patriot leaders and destroy their country with fire and sword. Such threats only made the mountain men all the more determined for a showdown with Ferguson.

While these events were taking place, Arthur Campbell was in Richmond where Governor Thomas Jefferson gave him the details of Gates' defeat. The two men discussed plans for an all-out effort to recoup the losses at Camden and to expel the British from the country. When he returned to Washington County, Campbell received a message from Colonel Isaac Shelby, the ranking officer in Sullivan County, North Carolina, informing him of Ferguson's progress and the retreat of McDowell's forces. The tale of McDowell's men, remarked Campbell, "was a doleful one, and tended to excite the resentment of the western militia, who of late had become inured to danger by fighting the Indians, and who had an utter detestation of the tyranny of the British government."[30] Shelby had already written William Campbell twice asking him to join John Sevier and himself in an expedition to stop Ferguson. William Campbell, thinking he could be of better service elsewhere, replied that he intended to march to the southern border of Virginia and oppose Cornwallis when he advanced from Charlotte.

When Arthur Campbell received Shelby's message, he immediately assured Shelby that the Washington County militia would cooperate with him in a march across the mountains. Campbell apparently discussed Jefferson's plans with William Campbell and convinced William he could best be of service to his country by joining Shelby and Sevier. At a meeting of the Washington

County field officers, September 22, 1780, it was decided that half the militia of the county under William Campbell would join the North Carolina militia. Arthur Campbell issued an order for the men and the quota was soon filled. Word was sent to Colonel Benjamin Cleveland of Wilkes County, North Carolina, to raise as many men as he could and to rendezvous with the Holston and Watauga men after they crossed the mountain.

William Campbell, with 200 men, and Shelby and Sevier with 100 men each, met McDowell with 150 men at Sycamore Shoals, September 25.[31] Just before they began their march across the mountains, the troops heard a noise in the distance and a few minutes later amidst shouts and cheers, Arthur Campbell marched in with an additional 200 men.[32] Arthur returned to Royal Oak, thus missing the campaign.

Among the other officers from Virginia, under William Campbell's command, were captains Gilbert Christian, James Shelby and William Edmiston, Jr.; lieutenants Robert Edmiston, Sr., John Houston and Thomas McCulloch; and ensigns Andrew Edmiston, James Houston, John McCutcheon, Abraham McClelland, and Josiah Ramsey. The army was joined by Cleveland and his men. Among the North Carolina men were Lt. Robert McFarland, William Cook, John and Mitchel Childers, James and Samuel Knox and many others. Additional men from South Carolina and Georgia raised the number of the Patriot Army to around 1,800. William Campbell was elected by his fellow officers to take command of the expedition.[33]

Roosevelt gives this description of the gathering of mountain men:

> Their fringe and tasseled hunting-shirts were girded by bead-worked belts, and the trappings of their horses were stained red and yellow. On their heads they wore caps of coon-skin or mink-skin, with the tails hanging down, or else felt hats, in each of which was thrust a buck's tail or a sprig of evergreen. Every man carried a small bore rifle, a tomahawk and a scalping knife. A very few of the officers had swords, and there was not a bayonet nor a tent in the army.[34]

The frontier was seriously weakened with so many of its best men going on the expedition. As county lieutenant, Arthur Campbell believed the responsibilities of his office required that he remain at home. Had he gone on the expedition it is quite likely that he would have been asked to take command of the mountain men and the fame and glory that William Campbell won at Kings Mountain, fought between the mountain men and Ferguson's forces on October 7, 1780, would have been his. But this was not the case and the important service he provided in protecting his own region and the services he rendered in organizing the Washington County militia for the Kings Mountain campaign has never been sufficiently recognized and appreciated.

On the sixth of October, it was decided to pick about 940 mounted riflemen, and after nightfall to pursue Ferguson, while the rest of the men followed as quickly as possible. Meanwhile, Charles McDowell left the mountain men in search of a Continental officer to command them. The next day, October 7, at three p.m., the Patriots caught up with Ferguson and his men, who were encamped on the top of Kings Mountain on the border of North and South Carolina. Ferguson boasted he could not be driven from such an advantageous position.

The Patriots quickly encircled the heavily shrubbed and wooded mountain and took their positions. Beginning with Colonel Campbell's regiment situated at the southwestern point of the mountain and moving counterclockwise, the other commanders and their regiments were Lieutenant Colonel Sevier, Major Joseph McDowell, Major Joseph Winston, Colonel Frederick Hambright, Colonel Cleveland, Colonel Edward Lacy, Colonel James Williams and Colonel Shelby. Major William Chronicle's men were positioned near Hambright's at the northeast side of the mountain.

Shelby's and Campbell's regiments began the attack as the right and left wings moved to completely surround Ferguson. Within five minutes all the regiments were pouring in fire, and by then the stunned British were returning the fire. Some of the Patriots were driven backward when the enemy charged them with fixed bayonets, but the patriots rallied and repulsed the Loyalists. When the right wing of the Patriot Army reached the summit, the enemy retreated but was stopped by Cleveland's men. Ferguson, mounted on horseback, and swinging his sword fiercely, attempted to break through, when six to eight bullets pierced his body, one striking him in the head. As he fell from the saddle his foot caught in the stirrup, his horse dragging him some distance until it was stopped.

After Ferguson was killed, Captain Abraham DePeyster, Ferguson's second in command, raised the flag of surrender, and after a time of confusion during which firing continued, the battle was over. It lasted about 55 minutes. British casualties numbered 225 killed, 130 wounded and about 700 taken prisoners. Twenty-eight Patriots were killed and 62 wounded. Among the Washington County men killed in the battle were William Edmiston, Jr., Robert Edmiston, Sr., and Andrew Edmiston.[35]

As soon as the Battle of Kings Mountain was over, both William Campbell and Isaac Shelby sent Arthur Campbell a report of the campaign.[36] In his memoirs, Arthur Campbell described the Battle of Kings Mountain and the significance of this event.

> On the twenty-eighth [26th] of September our little army took up its line of march, and the third day in the evening reached the other side, without any opposition from the enemy. Two days afterwards, Colonel Cleveland joined his corps to the main body; and the day afterwards Colonel Williams, with three companies of volunteers from South Carolina. A council of officers was held, and it was agreed that Colonel William Campbell, of Virginia, should take command of the whole, and pursue the enemy. Colonel Ferguson, after dispersing such parties of the North Carolina militia as were embodied, followed Colonel McDowell's men as far as the foot of the great mountains, and after taking some prisoners, and collecting a drove of beeves, he made a hasty retreat to Kings Mountain, in order to be nearer the main army, and on account of the strong encampment that might be formed on the top of it. Our newly elected commander reviewed his men, and selected all that were fit for service of the mounted infantry, and ordered the footmen to follow as they might be able to hold out. . . .
>
> . . .[O]ur heroes had to act as a forlorn hope—stormed the enemy's camp defended by superior numbers and disciplined troops . . . It was Ferguson's defeat that was the first link in a grand chain of causes, which finally drew down ruin on the British interests in the Southern States, and finally terminated the war of the Revolution. . .[37]

More recent authorities, Hugh Talmage Lefler and Albert Ray Newsome, note that "Kings Mountain was a remarkable military feat by undisciplined militia, under neither state nor Continental control.... [W]eakened by the loss of his left wing and robbed of his confidence in North Carolina loyalism, Cornwallis abandoned his plans and fled with great precipitation from Charlotte to Winnsboro, South Carolina...."[38] Another scholar of the American Revolution, Henry Lumpkin, asserts that Kings Mountain "could be called the first major step in the ... campaign that led to Cornwallis's surrender at Yorktown and the final expulsion of the British from Georgia and the Carolinas."[39]

Victorious, the mountain men returned to their homes to face the threat of a Cherokee invasion of the Holston and Watauga settlements. Early in December it was generally assumed that the Cherokee and Chickamaugas, under the leadership of Dragging Canoe and Oconostota, would soon began an all out war. Small parties had been seen near the settlements and Campbell was convinced that the whites could expect nothing but war from the Indians, and unless the war was first carried into the Indian's own country, many families would be killed on the frontier. The Wataugans were especially apprehensive since they were near the Indian country, and Sevier, like Campbell, was determined to carry the war to the Indians.[40]

Campbell met with the officers at Watauga and it appears that he planned and assumed the command of a joint Virginia-Carolina operation into the Indian country. After the meeting he told William Campbell that "the officers of Carolina seemed well inclined to have everything conducted with regularity and readily acquiesced with proposals I made them. I can see no better method now to defend the country from the depredation of the enemy." He ordered all the men of Washington County who were fit for service to report for duty with at least ten days' provisions for themselves and a bushel of corn for each horse. Each company was also to be equipped with two small axes or a few tomahawks. It was, however, extremely difficult to raise a sufficient force and equip them properly at this time of the year, but when they were reminded of the miseries of 1776, the men rallied to the cause.[41]

Sevier was to provide some 300 men. Joseph Martin of Sullivan County, North Carolina, and Campbell's combined force amounted to about 400 more. These forces were supposed to rendezvous at the French Broad River, but Sevier began to march before the others reached the river. At Boyd's Creek on December 16, he engaged a party of Indians, killing 13 of them. Among the things found on the Indians after the engagement were some of General Henry Clinton's proclamations and other documents concerning British and Indian plans against the Patriots.[42] Sevier returned to the French Broad with his men who, because they had not been properly equipped, were exhausted and hungry. On December 22, Campbell crossed the river and provided them with rations and the next day the combined force marched toward the Tennessee River.

Campbell's army approached the Tennessee River with anxiety. It was reported that the Indians were waiting in force to block a crossing. On the morning of the 24th, Campbell made it appear as if he were heading for Island Town (also called Dragging Canoe Town) but then took the main body of troops across at "Timotlee" without resistance.

Once across the Tennessee River Campbell's men saw the Indians in apparent flight. Here he divided his force, sending one part to attack the lower towns and the other to the principle town of Chote. All along the hills below Chote the Indians could be seen, but they refused to attack, firing only a few shots at Campbell's rear guard. Chote was easily taken and they found a welcomed supply of provisions there. The next day Major Joseph Martin took a detachment of troops to determine the Indians' route of escape. He surprised a party, took one scalp and 17 horses loaded with clothing, skins, and furniture. Martin then discovered that the Indians were fleeing toward Telico and Hiwassee. One of the Virginia officers was sent with 60 men to burn the town of Chilhowee. Attacked by a large force of warriors, he was forced to retreat after burning only part of the town. On the 26th, Major Jonathan Tipton led 150 mounted infantry across the river in an unsuccessful attempt to dislodge the enemy and destroy Talasee. Major Gilbert Christian took 150 men on foot to patrol the hills on the south side of Chilhowee. They killed three Indians, took nine prisoners and burned the town.

Following the destructive raids, Nancy Ward, the Indian woman who for years had offered friendly assistance to the whites, came to Campbell and reported that some of the chiefs wanted to talk peace. Since the Indian campaign was going so well Campbell avoided giving her an explicit answer, hoping to inflict heavier punishment on the Indians, particularly those at Hiwassee and Chistowee. This he was able to do. On December 28, he burned Chote, Scitigo, and Tuskeego, then moved with his entire force to a town on the Telico River called Kaiatee. Here he provided a place to insure a safe retreat if necessary, and to store provisions.

The following day Campbell set out for Hiwassee, a distance of about 40 miles. He arrived on the 30th and found the town abandoned. A young warrior captured in the vicinity informed Campbell that a body of Indians, a British agent by the name of McDonald, and some Tories were waiting for him at Chistowee, 12 miles from Hiwassee. Realizing that his movements could be observed from the hills, he ordered fires built to give the appearance that he would remain in camp all night.

That night Campbell and about 300 men crossed the river and marched toward Chistowee; his force was weakened somewhat when Sevier's men refused to go further. Early on the morning of the 31st he arrived at the town, but again the Indians were not to be found. They had left behind all their corn, livestock, furniture, and agricultural implements.

By now Campbell's men were becoming exhausted and it was decided to withdraw from the Indian country. On their way home, Campbell ordered Major Martin to proceed to Sattoga and the other towns on the Telico River, where he learned that several of the chiefs had met to determine a means of obtaining peace.[43] The chiefs were sent the following message:

> Chiefs and Warriors: We came into your country to fight your young men. We have killed not a few of them and destroyed your towns. You know you began the war, by listening to the bad councils of the King of England and the falsehoods told you by his agents. We are now satisfied with what is done, as it may convince your nation that we can distress them much at any time they are so foolish as to engage in a war against us. If you desire peace, as we understand you do, we, out of pity to your women and children, are disposed to treat with you on that subject and take you into our friendship once more. We therefore send this by one of

your young men, who is our prisoner, to tell you if you are also disposed to make peace, for six of your head men to come to our agent, Major Martin, at the Great Island within two moons. They will have a safe passport, if they will notify us of their approach by a runner with a flag, so as to give him time to meet them with a guard on Holstein [sic] River, at the boundary line. The wives and children of these men of your nation that protested against the war, if they are willing to take refuge at the Great Island until peace is restored, we will give them a supply of provisions to keep them alive.

Warriors listen attentively.

If we receive no answer to this message until the time already mentioned expires, we shall conclude you intend to continue to be our enemies, which will compel us to send another strong force into your country who will come prepared to stay a long time, and take possession thereof, as conquered by us, without making any restitution to you for your lands.

Signed at Kai-a-tee the 4th day of January, one thousand seven hundred and eighty-one by

> Arthur Campbell, Col.
> John Sevier, Lieutenant-Col.
> Joseph Martin, Agent &
> Major of Militia[44]

The chiefs responded by meeting Martin at Chote, and although nothing important was accomplished at this meeting, no major battle was fought from this point on, for the Indians fled as Campbell approached.

Campbell has been credited with introducing a new method of fighting the Indian during the campaign by attacking them with mounted riflemen, "an experiment which proved entirely successful."[45] Only one of the militia was killed while Indian losses were 29 killed and 17 captured, mostly women and children. Among the Indians brought back to the Holston settlements was the family of Nancy Ward, who was well treated because of her loyalty to the whites. While the number of enemy killed was not large, the destruction to their towns was staggering. The towns of Chote, Scittigo, Chilhowee, Togue, Michiqua, Kai-a-tee, Sattoogo, Telico, Hiwassee, and Chistowee, all principle towns and a few small ones, were destroyed. For the Indians this meant the loss of over 1,000 houses, about 50,000 bushels of corn, and large quantities of additional provisions. Only the small towns of Telafee and Caloogee in the Overhill Country were left unmolested by Campbell's forces.[46]

When Campbell returned to Royal Oak he sent Jefferson a detailed report of the expedition. Campbell was under no illusions concerning the results of the campaign, although he believed the Cherokees would promise peace. To keep the Cherokee Nation in a pacified state, however, he recommended that a permanent garrison be stationed at the confluence of the Tennessee and Holston rivers.[47] Jefferson seemed to favor the idea, but told Campbell the matter would have to be referred to the Continental Congress because the site was beyond Virginia's border.[48] Campbell had to settle for authority to build a fort at Cumberland Gap, which was constructed largely to protect the settlers going to Kentucky.[49]

About a month after Arthur Campbell's expedition against the Indians, General Nathanael Greene appointed him, William Christian, William Preston and Joseph Martin of Virginia, and Robert and John Sevier, Evan Shelby and Joseph Williams of North Carolina, to negotiate a treaty with the Cherokees. There was to be an adjustment of the boundary between the Indians and the white men, an exchange of prisoners, a suspension of hostilities, and "anything else for the establishment of harmony...."[50] While Campbell thought a treaty was desirable, he suggested that peace would best be obtained by again "terrifying the perfidous tribe...."[51] He did not believe there could be peace with the southern Indians as long as Augusta, Georgia, was held by the British, for the town was a base of supply for the Indians.[52] However, William Christian may have seen the situation more clearly. "The only great inducements the Indians can have for treating," he wrote Jefferson, "are for us to do them justice respecting their lands and to subsist their families this summer."[53]

Representatives from the Cherokee towns met at Long Island, located at the forks of the Holston and Watauga rivers, July 20, 1781, and a peace agreement was reached. Campbell doubted the sincerity of the Indians and thought their conduct might "merit them further correction before long."[54] He was correct, for fighting continued with the Cherokees, and North Carolina sent an expedition to destroy their towns.

The continued conflict with the Indians greatly limited the assistance the West could give the East. Had it not been for this the Revolutionary War might have ended much sooner. The Battle of Kings Mountain illustrates what the mountain men could do when freed from responsibilities at home, but this was a rare occasion. In February, 1781, Jefferson, preparing for Cornwallis, contacted Campbell and other county lieutenants in the back country for reinforcements. Jefferson informed the county lieutenants that the British general was pressing toward Virginia and Greene was retreating before him. Jefferson urgently asked the officers to send half of their militia to Greene.[55] Campbell was faced with the Indian danger at home and his men were not eager to leave their homes. The fact that they had not been paid for past services also contributed to their unwillingness to comply with Jefferson's orders. Consequently, Campbell could send only 60 of his militia. This was extremely disappointing to Greene, who expected far more. Campbell explained to Jefferson that "a larger number would have gone were it not for the daily apprehensions of attacks from the northward and southern Indians...."[56] Three months later Jefferson again requested that Campbell send Greene reinforcements. But Campbell was forced to write the governor that he was "very sorry our situation at present is such that I have but small prospect of forwarding the aid required...." Pressuring Jefferson for money to pay his militia, Campbell added that he could probably send reinforcements if his men were paid the money the government owed them.[57] Jefferson received similar replies from other county lieutenants.[58]

While he could provide but few reinforcements to the East, Campbell was sending men and supplies to Kentucky, as conditions there were considered more desperate.[59] Early in June, 1780, Campbell received word from Colonel John Bowman that a British officer with 600 regulars and 1,000 Indians were about to attack the post at the Falls of the Ohio.[60] The British captain, Henry Byrd, who was to lead the attack, wrote his superior officer at Detroit that the "Indians have their full spirits, the ammunition, and everything plenty, and in the state we would wish it."[61] Campbell sent three companies of militia to Kentucky to be used in defense of the Falls or wherever they could best be of service.[62] The attack never materialized. The Indian, afraid they might have to face George Rogers Clark, preferred instead to strike the smaller settlements at Hinkston and Ruddell forts.[63]

The situation in Kentucky grew increasingly worse the following year. John Floyd, county lieutenant of Kentucky County, vividly described the situation to Jefferson.

> Whole families are destroyed, without regard to age or sex. Infants are torn from their mother's arms and their brains dashed out against trees, as they are necessarily removing from one fort to another for safety or convenience. Not a week passes and some weeks scarcely a day without some of our distressed inhabitants feeling the fatal effects of the infernal rage and fury of those Execrable hell hounds.
>
> Our garrisons are dispersed over an extensive country, and a large proportion of the inhabitants are helpless, indigent widows and orphans, who have lost their husbands and fathers by savage hands, and left among strangers, without the most common necessaries of life. Of those who have escaped, many have lost all their stocks, and have not any land of their own, nor where withal to purchase. Our dependence to support our familys is upon getting wild meat and this is procured with great difficulty and danger; and should it fall to the lott of some of this county who are thus situated to serve as regular soldiers according to law, their families must inevitably starve.[64]

In the winter of 1781 Clark wrote Governor Harrison of Virginia that he had received alarming accounts from Detroit that in the spring the enemy would "lay the whole country [of Kentucky] to waste...."[65] By midsummer a large force of British and northwestern tribes gathered in the Shawnee country under captains William Caldwell and Alexander McKee, preparing to attack the fort at the Falls. According to McKee this was "the greatest body of Indians ... that have been assembled in this quarter since the commencement of war, and perhaps never may be in higher spirits to attack the enemy."[66]

When the Indians again learned that they might have to fight Clark the Shawnees refused to go on the campaign. The British, however, persuaded over 300 Hurons and Great Lakes Indians to attack Bryan's Station in Fayette County, August 16. They burned a few houses and fought for two days and then retreated with the

Kentuckians in pursuit. At Blue Licks the Indians set up an ambush. Some 180 Kentuckians under Colonel John Todd and Stephen Trigg, fell into the trap. After five minutes of close fighting the Kentuckians were routed. Sixty-six of the militia, including Todd and Trigg, were killed. According to Temple Bodley, "this was the greatest disaster that had befallen the Kentuckian people during the entire war...."[67]

The blame for the Blue Licks disaster was placed on George Rogers Clark, although he was not within a hundred miles and did not even know about the affair. The accusers pointed out that Clark should have built a fort at the Licking, that he should have been in the area, and a dozen other accusations. Colonel Benjamin Logan, county lieutenant of Lincoln, wrote the governor of Virginia implying that the responsibility rested with Clark. Other military and civil officers in Kentucky also blamed Clark. Arthur Campbell, who at this time was in the Virginia Assembly, joined in the criticism of Clark, pointing out to Colonel William Davies that Clark "has lost the confidence of the people and, it is said, become a sot; perhaps something worse."[68] Campbell was probably quite happy to pass this word along and what he said was at least partially true. Clark has lost the confidence of some of the back-country people; but it was because he did not join the new state movement developing there rather than any military deficiency he might have had.

The brunt of Campbell's charge as to who bore responsibility for the Blue Licks disaster fell on Major Hugh McGary, who had broken up a separatist meeting at Harrodsburg which Campbell had helped to organize. "Never," wrote Campbell, "was the lives of so many valuable men lost more shamefully than in the late action of the 19th of August and that not a little through the vain and seditious expression of a Major McGarry [sic]. How much more harm than good can one fool do...."[69] Vindictive comments such as these circulated around Richmond and did much to distort conditions in Kentucky and destroy the reputation of military officials there.

Despited his personal feelings, Campbell showed a clear understanding of the situation in the West. He believed that the British were "uniting the savage tribes and endeavoring to sow the seeds of deep laid animosity, which will lengthen the Indian war to a longer period than most imagine." What was needed, according to Campbell, was "a decided blow in the enemy country." Before this could happen, he pointed out, new methods of warfare should be introduced, such as the bayonet and scythe, and "evolutions suited to the woods should be learned both by foot and horse."[70]

Meanwhile, the dramatic change in the military situation in the East postponed the necessity for a "decided blow" in the West. Nathanael Greene, Daniel Morgan and Francis Marion made Cornwallis very uncomfortable in the months following the battle of Kings Mountain. On January 17, 1781, the Patriots won another important victory at Cowpens, South Carolina. In front of a tree-covered ridge Morgan positioned Maryland light infantry, Virginia riflemen and militia from the Carolinas and Georgia. Behind the ridge Morgan placed William Washington's light dragoons. No doubt these men, like those at Kings Mountain, were thinking about the unnecessary slaughter of Virginians at Waxhaw, South Carolina, at the hands of Tarleton. When Tarleton ordered a cavalry charge, the battle of Cowpens began. After a brief but bloody battle, the British commander withdrew, leaving 100 of his men dead and 829 prisoners.

Two months after the battle of Cowpens, Cornwallis won a costly battle at Guilford Court House, North Carolina. By the spring of 1781, he had reached Virignia, where he took command of a combined British force. In September he was at Yorktown, but so was the Continental Army under the personal command of Washington and a French army under the command of Rochambeau. On September 28, the battle of Yorktown began. With a French fleet commanded by Admiral de Grasse preventing his escape, Cornwallis was forced to surrender his 8,000 man army on October 19.[71] As the Red Coats stacked their arms the British band played "The World Turned Upside Down."

> If buttercups buzzed after the bee;
> If boats were on land, churches on sea;
> If ponies rode men, and grass ate the cow;
> If cats should be chased into holes by the mouse;
> If mammas sold their babies to Gypsies for half a crown;

If summer were spring and the other way round;
Then all the world would be upside down.[72]

What an appropriate song! The impossible was a reality. America had won its independence and in the Treaty of Paris of 1783 the British government officially accepted this fact.

The Battle of Blue Licks was the last British effort to take Kentucky. In the South, the Cherokees, who had suffered much at the hands of Campbell, Shelby and Sevier, were pushed farther southwest, as the horde of whites poured into the upper Tennessee country. While the Indians remained a serious problem and scattered fighting on the frontier continued, the great threat which Campbell and the people of Washington County faced for so long was passing.

6 The Greater State of Franklin

By the terms of the Treaty of Paris of 1783, George III acknowledged the United States "to be free, sovereign and independent. . . ." The boundaries of the new nation were roughly the Great Lakes to the north, the Mississippi River to the west, and in the South, the thirty-first degree of north latitude. Spain regained Florida in a separate treaty with England.[1]

Independence brought with it what appeared to be insurmountable problems for the United States, some of which arose over what land policies would be implemented in the vast territory acquired from England and who would have the authority to establish those policies. Thus, the controversies raging before the Revolution concerning western lands did not end with American independence.

During the Confederation era, 1781–1789, frontier people living great distances from their state capitals often demanded that the seats of government be moved closer to the back country, and they also insisted on a stronger voice in the new state governments. East-west conflicts were not new, as Bacon's Rebellion in Virginia and the Regulator movements in North Carolina and South Carolina in the late 1760s and early 1770s clearly reveal, but the problems increased as a result of the war.

In an attempt to pacify the westerners, some states' capitals were moved westward: in South Carolina the capital was changed from Charleston to Columbia, in North Carolina from New Bern

73

to Raleigh, in Georgia from Savannah to Augusta, and in Virginia from Williamsburg to Richmond.[2] Some back country people were not satisfied with such limited concession, demanding instead that new states be created out of territory within the boundaries of the older states. In the South the most serious conflicts over new state movements arose in Virginia and North Carolina.

Arthur Campbell was the recognized leader of the new state movement in Southwest Virginia and North Carolina, and greatly influenced the movement in Kentucky. "In the brain of this virile and strong-willed man, possessed of Scotch Irish initiative, courage and tenacity," wrote Samuel Cole Williams, "was formed the first conception of a separate state for the sturdy population . . . in southwestern Virginia and the . . . settlements to the south in North Carolina."[3]

Before the conclusion of the war the Continental Congress resolved that if the states of Virginia, North Carolina and Georgia complied with its request to cede a portion of their unappropriated western land, "the territory so ceded shall be laid out in separate . . . states at such times and in such manner as Congress shall hereafter direct."[4] Another resolution of the Congress stated that new states would have the "same rights of sovereignty, freedom and in- dependence as the other states."[5]

When Arthur Campbell heard about the national land policy he became very interested in the possibility of a new state in Southwest Virginia that would eventually include parts of West Virginia, Kentucky, western North Carolina, Alabama, Tennessee and Georgia. In 1782, with some assistance from Colonel William Christian, brother-in-law of Patrick Henry, he began devising a plan for obtaining the attitude of the people of the southwest con- cerning the possibility of creating a new state.[6]

The people of western North Carolina were not unlike those of Southwest Virginia, living under the same fears of Indian attacks and sharing similar grievances against their state governments. They were, in short, divided only by the boundary line that separated the two states. Little wonder, then, that Campbell wrote John Sevier at Watauga on January 21, 1782, explaining his ideas.[7] It is not surprising either that Sevier responded favorably to the plan of a separate state. On February 16, Sevier wrote:

[C]oncerning our new western world . . . I have thought much on the subject of late. I am sorry I live so remote that I cannot have an opportunity of discussing Matters with Gentlemen Wiser in Politics than myself, but nevertheless, I shall Beg leave to say something on this Important Subject, I Hope without giving offense. . . .

If Congress have officially assumed the right of the Western Country as I Suggest from your Letter I must Coincide with you that a meeting of select men ought immediately to be & the people at Large [be] as fully Represented as Possible. I must believe it to be a matter of great Importance & Exceedingly Interesting to our Western Country & we ought to be attentive – It is very evident That our settling this Country Hitherto has been through many difficulties and with the loss of many good Citizens, Our different possessions have been occupied through Many and Various Hazards and Chiefly occasioned by our Remote situation from the seats of government. Therefore I must think it would be a prudent step To endeavour to throw off some of those predicaments we Have so Long groaned [under] & as all political Authority Originates with the Collective Body, we undoubtedly ought to Have a meeting but by what way and means [I] shall not pretend to say. but leave it for some Greater politician to Adopt – Colo. Selby Informed me That some plan was on foot & at our Court Would furnish me with a Copy if she should Receive one in time. [Our] Similar predicaments are nearly the same & I shall always be glad to cooperate with you in Business of this Nature In anything I can be serviceable in to The public Good. I shall always be Happy to hear from you, & am much Ablidged to you for the several letters. . . .[8]

The details of the plan to determine the attitude of the western inhabitants toward a separate state, formulated by Campbell and Christian, were circulated in the western counties in the form of a document. This document, directed toward the people of Southwest Virginia and western North Carolina, was, according to Samuel Cole Williams, the genesis of the state of Franklin, which was created from the western counties of North Carolina.[9] The plan consisted of five steps:

> 1st. That Selectmen or Deputies be chosen for the five southwestern counties of Virginia and the counties of Washington and Sullivan in North Carolina to meet at Abingdon the third Wednesday in April, 1782.

2nd. That in order that the representation be adequate, let the Deputies be in number proportionate to the number of farmers above eighteen years of age, allowing one Deputy for every hundred such farmers.

3rd. That the election be held at the respective Court Houses on the third Tuesday in the month of March next, by the same officers and under the same regulations as elections for delegates are held.

4th. The business and power of Deputies when convened to be the consideration of the late Resolves of Congress respecting the Western Country, and to adopt such measures as may be adjudged proper by a majority for the interest and safety of their constituents as members of the American Union.

5th. The representation to continue one year, in which time the Deputies may adjourn from time to time and to such places within the western counties as may be found most convenient.[10]

An election was held in Washington County, Virginia, for delegates, who met late in 1782 or early 1783. At one of their meetings the Assembly drew up an address to the people of Washington County signed by the chairman, Charles Cummings, a popular Presbyterian minister in the County. While Cummings signed it, Arthur Campbell was the most actively involved in explaining and championing its ideas.[11]

It was argued that the laws of Virginia, particularly the tax laws, were unfair to the people of the West. "If your eastern neighbors were generous," states the address, "they would make some allowance for the great losses sustained by the depredations of the Indians, and for the many valuable lives lost to keep them safe...." In anticipation of Virginia's opposition to the separatist movement, the people were urged to disregard the "impotent threats," of their "rulers," in the East and to stand up for their rights.[12] Meetings were held throughout the county to discuss the issues raised by the plan and Campbell was vocal at these meetings elaborating on the tax issue and urging the inhabitants to refuse to pay their taxes.[13]

Campbell was very busy in 1782 and 1783 formulating and publicizing his separate state ideas. His hopes were intensified by Congress which was pressuring Virginia to give up its western land. On June 9, 1782, he wrote a member of the Confederation Congress, Arthur Lee of Virginia, expressing his thoughts as to what the new state might encompass. He expected that the Ohio River would become the western boundary of the new state, but if that were not the case then a line should be drawn in such a way as to enable Montgomery and Washington counties in Virginia to join with the people of North Carolina residing on the heads of the Tennessee "and have in contemplation a new state in that beautiful valley of which the Cherokees are yet the principle possessors."[14] It is clear from this letter that as early as the spring of 1782 Campbell was anticipating the time when the western counties of Virginia and North Carolina would create a separate state, but he also understood that in order for such a state to succeed, support from the Continental Congress was imperative. During this same time, he was also interested in the separate state movement in Kentucky, where separatist there were also petitioning Congress for support.[15]

When Virginia ceded its western lands to the Continental Congress in 1783, no doubt Campbell was very disappointed that the cession did not include Southwest Virginia. Nevertheless, he became even more determined to carry out his plans for a separate state. As could be expected, a party emerged in opposition to him. This group was led by Colonel William Russell who, as is often the case, had personal as well as political differences with Campbell. Like Campbell, Russell was a well known figure in Washington County. He had settled near Castle's Woods on the Clinch River in 1770, and commanded a company of men at the Battle of Point Pleasant. Along with Campbell, he was chosen to represent Fincastle County at the Virginia Convention and the General Assembly in 1776. When William Campbell died in August, 1781, Russell married his widow, Elizabeth, the sister of Patrick Henry.

The new Mrs. Russell apparently never liked Arthur Campbell, perhaps because she was jealous that William Campbell did not acquire the prestige in Southwest Virginia that his cousin Arthur did. This was true despite William's accomplishments at Kings Mountain. The situation might have been different had William not died of pneumonia less than a year after the historic battle. Based on William's will, a court order was issued on March 21, 1783, giving Arthur Campbell and William Christian guardianship of William Campbell's children, a common occurrence which would cause a later generation of women to rise up in outrage. From that time on dissension increased. Arthur's dogmatic determination to execute his cousin's will, and especially his concern for the welfare of William's daughter, Sarah, caused many heated arguments which had to be settled in court.

Mrs. Russell's dislike of Arthur was matched only by that of her husband's, who could now use political reasons to "get" Arthur Campbell. In September, 1783, Russell wrote Governor Benjamin Harrison expressing his fear that "Col. Campbell's present close attention to affect a new state in this part of the country will engage his time to the neglect [of his duties as a judge]...."[16] This was just the beginning of a crusade on Russell's part to remove Campbell from positions of power and prestige in Washington County. It is obvious, however, that Russell spoke for a minority since Campbell was popular enough to be elected to the General Assembly for a third time in 1783.[17]

In April, 1784, Congress adopted Jefferson's resolutions for creating new states out of ceded land in the west. Among the provisions of the resolution was one stating: "The settlers on any territory [ceded] ... shall, either on their own petition or on the order of Congress, receive authority..." to create new states following the procedures outlined by Congress. The point is that after the adoption of Jefferson's resolutions it was commonly assumed that the inhabitants on land no longer claimed by the states, were perfectly free to create new states, and as the resolutions indicated, these newly created states would be equal in every way to the old ones.[18]

The same month that Congress adopted Jefferson's plan for the organization of governments in the western territory, the North Carolina Assembly approved an act ceding its westernmost counties to the Confederation Congress. The main reason for giving up this vast area, the future state of Tennessee, was to reduce North Carolina's share of the financial burden of the war, in the event that Congress passed a tax law based on each state's population and the amount of land it possessed.[19]

After the passage of the Cession Act the frontier settlers of North Carolina, feeling they had been abandoned by their state, joined the Virginians already active in a new state movement. In accordance with Arthur Campbell's plan an election for deputies to a general convention was held. Delegates from the counties of Sullivan, Greene and Washington, North Carolina, met at Jonesboro, August 24, 1784. Davidson County did not participate. The delegates chose John Sevier president of the Convention and created a committee which unanimously approved a resolution declaring the three counties of Washington, Sullivan, and Greene independent of North Carolina.

The committee submitted its decision on independence to the convention in the form of a report. The report, also approved by the convention, 28 to 15, stated they had "a just and undeniable right to petition to Congress to accept the cession made by North Carolina and for that body to countenance us in forming ourselves into a separate government...." The report went on to assert that "When any contiguous part of Virginia shall make application to join this association, after they are legally permitted, either by the State of Virginia, or other power [the Confederation Congress] ... it is our opinion that they be received and enjoy the same privileges that we do, may or shall enjoy."[20] This statement made it plain that Arthur Campbell's plan for a state which would include Southwest Virginia and western North Carolina had been favorably received by the separatists of North Carolina.

After a second convention in November, 1784, broke up in confusion when the delegates could hardly agree on anything, a third met in Jonesboro December 14. This convention elected Sevier president and approved a plan of association drawn up by William Cocke and Joseph Hardin, in which were stated the advantages of a separate state, and why it was necessary for a separation. It was noted that the population in the new state would quickly increase, bringing with it an increase in the amount of gold and silver in circulation. Agriculture and industry would be enhanced as would education, and in other ways, too, the quality of life for the western people would greatly improve. On the other hand, these improvements could not take place as long as the West remained attached to the East, for the eastern counties, being the most numerous, would always be able to make the West subservient to them. It was stated that the West's interest would be neglected and even sacrificed to promote the interest of the East. The separatists also complained of an unfair and burdensome tax law recently passed. These were the reasons for a separation and, therefore, the delegates agreed to protect the Association with their lives and fortunes, "to which we pledge our faith and reputations."[21]

The convention adopted a provisional constitution modelled after the Constitution of North Carolina and the new state was named "Franklin," in honor of Benjamin Franklin. Williams, in *The Lost State of Franklin*, points out that the constitution was unique in form in that it was prefaced by a "Declaration of Independence" and a "bill of rights," under the title "Declaration of the State of Franklin." The bill of rights was written by Arthur Campbell, according to Summers in his *History of Southwest Virginia*.[22] Concerning this convention, David Campbell wrote his brother Arthur, "We had a convention, and whether wrong or right they have brought matters to a crisis, they have declared this country a separate and independent state by the name of 'Franklin'...."[23]

By the time the third convention convened, North Carolina had already repealed the Cession Act. The reason for this turn-around, as stated in the Act of Repeal, was

> ...the cession, so intended was made in full confidence that the whole expense of the Indian expeditions and military aids to the states of South Carolina and Georgia should pass to account in our quota of the continental expenses in the late war, and also that the other states would unanimously grant imposts of five per cent as a common fund for the discharge of the federal debt; and whereas the states of Massachusetts and Connecticut, after accepting the cessions of New York and Virginia, have since put in claims for a large part of that territory, all the above expected measures for constituting a substantial common fund have either been frustrated or delayed.[24]

During the same session of the North Carolina Assembly, steps were taken to alleviate some of the grievances of the frontier people. The four western counties were formed into a judicial district called Washington. John Sevier was appointed brigadier-general and David Campbell was made superior court judge of Washington District.[25]

After North Carolina repealed its Cession Act some of the Franklinites, including Sevier, wanted to rejoin the mother state.

Sevier, who claimed he had been dragged into the separatist movement from its beginning, wrote his friend, Colonel Daniel Kennedy,

> I have just received certain information from Colonel Martin that the first thing the Assembly of North Carolina did, was to repeal the cession bill, and to form this part of the country into a separate District, by the name of Washington District, which I have the honor to command. I conclude this step will satisfy the people with the old State and we shall pursue no further measures as to a new State.[26]

According to Sevier's biographer, Sevier actually began to discourage the creation of a new state because he was afraid it would interfere with the Muscle Shoals speculating project he was involved in. But the success of Muscle Shoals depended on frontier support and when it became apparent that the Franklin movement had advanced too far to be easily ended, Sevier joined the separatists.[27]

Campbell was carrying on a vigorous campaign in Virginia during this time, trying to get the western counties to join the State of Franklin. When he was asked if he would be willing to go to the aid of Franklin if North Carolina sent a force against it, Campbell answered that "we ought, by all means, if we expect to share with them the advantages of their government."[28] On another occasion he assured a group of Franklinites that he "proposed to separate himself with the citizens of Washington and Montgomery in Virginia, and joining them, declare themselves immediately independent of the states of Virginia and North Carolina, and moreover stand [in] the front of the battle between these people and Virginia when necessary."[29] To a Virginia audience he vowed that before he would live under such a government [as Virginia's] he would take his musket on his shoulder and fight until he lost the last drop of blood in his body...."[30]

The Franklinites disregarded the repeal of the Cession Act and held their first General Assembly in March, 1785, at Jonesboro. Sevier, who did not leave the movement, was elected governor, Landon Carter, speaker of the Senate, and William Gage, speaker of the House; David Campbell became a justice of the Superior Court. Daniel Kennedy and William Cocke were appointed brigadier-generals of the militia. The assembly created the counties of Spencer, Caswell, Sevier and Wayne, the latter to be erected from part of Washington County (North Carolina) and "that part of Wilkes lying west of the extreme heights of the Appalachian . . . Mountains."[31]

The second session of the Franklin Assembly called for a constitutional convention to draw up a permanent frame of government for the State of Franklin. The convention convened in Greenville, November 14, 1785. Arthur Campbell greatly influenced the proceedings of the convention. A constitution which he and the Reverend William Graham, president of Liberty Hall College, Lexington, Virginia, helped draw up was presented to the convention.[32] This was the first original constitution west of the mountains and according to Thomas P. Abernethy was in "many respects one of the most democratic ever produced in the United States."[33] It was championed at the convention by the Reverend Samuel Houston, who had received a degree from Liberty Hall College, and was strongly opposed by the Reverend Hezekiah Balch, also a former student of Liberty Hall. There was heated debate over the document and pamphlets were published for and against it.[34]

Abernethy notes that the Campbell party's constitution has been referred to as the fanatical propositions of a few clergymen, for it possessed so obviously the "ecclesiastical mark." It provided that office-holders must possess good character and believe in the Bible, the Trinity and the Protestant religion, but there was to be no established church, and freedom of worship was assured. The North Carolina Constitution required the same religious qualifications but omitted reference to character.[35] It further provided for a "one house legislature, manhood suffrage, voting by ballot, and referendum of all laws to the people before final passage." The governor was to be elected by the people as were the council and county officials. Taxes were to be set aside for the building and support of a university.[36]

Merrill Jensen maintains that "Sevier and eastern speculators behind him were afraid of what might happen if such a document were adopted."[37] "What might happen," meant the adoption of the Campbell constitution might result in too much democracy. Sevier was afraid that the people might acquire too powerful a voice in the public lands policies. Sevier, "a representative and agent of the speculators," was able to get the North Carolina Constitution adopted in place of the one proposed by the Campbell group. The North Carolina Constitution, although "democratic compared with some of the other state constitutions, . . . was thoroughly conservative compared with the constitution proposed by the followers of Arthur Campbell."[38]

Alexander Martin, governor of North Carolina, became alarmed when, after the repeal of the Cession Act, the Franklinites continued their separate state activities. On February 27, 1785, Martin wrote Sevier that "with some concern I have heard that the counties of Washington, Sullivan, and Greene, have declared themselves independent of the state of North Carolina, and have chosen you governor. . . ." Martin went on to say:

> As I wish to have full and proper information on this subject . . .
> you will please to transmit me an account of the late proceedings
> of the people. . . . The general discontent that prevailed through
> the state at the late cession act, and the sense of Congress to make
> the state no retaliation for the same, caused the assembly to repeal
> the act . . . and to convince the people of the western country, that
> the state still retained her affection for them, was not desirous to
> part with so respectable a body of citizens, in the present situation
> of affairs, attempted to render government as easy as possible by
> erecting a new superior court district, creating a brigadier general
> of the militia, and an assistant judge of the said superior court,
> which was, in short, redressing every grievance, and removing
> every obstacle that called for a separation, and which the
> legislature were taught to believe . . . would give full satisfaction.[39]

The General Assembly of the State of Franklin was not impressed with Martin's letter. The assembly's frank reply is perhaps the best brief summary of the grievances of the Western people which had led to the creation of the State of Franklin in the first place. The letter stated ". . . we humbly thank North Carolina for every sentiment of regard she has for us, but are sorry to observe, that as it is founded up on principle of interest, as is apparent from the tenor of your letter, we are doubtful when the cause ceases which is the basis of that affection we shall lose your esteem."

The Franklinites reminded the governor of the language of some of the members of North Carolina general assembly at the time the Cession Act was being debated by quoting assembly members' words when referring to the frontier people as the "off-scourings of the earth; fugitives from justice; and we will be rid of them at any rate." They also reminded Martin that they had been left on their own by the Cession Act, which made them even more vulnerable to Indian attacks. Consequently, the people of the western counties organized as best they could for their own protection. Two other issues were pointed out, one being what amounted to a prohibition of the administration of justice, because of the great distance judges had to travel, and the other, the unfair tax system. Not only was the tax base inequitable but, they also argued, "the people of the western counties found themselves taxed to support government, while they were deprived of all the blessings of it."

The Franklinites closed their letter by asserting that:

> We are induced to think North Carolina will not blame us for endeavoring to promote our own interest and happiness, while we do not attempt to abridge her's, & appeal to the impartial world to determine, whether we have deserted North Carolina or North Carolina deserted us. You will please lay these our sentiments before the General Assembly....[40]

At that point Governor Martin, believing a much stronger position must be taken against the Franklinites, issued a manifesto on April 25, 1785, informing the western people that their grievances had been addressed and warned them to cease their separate state activities.[41]

In response to the governor's manifesto, Sevier issued a proclamation in which he accused the governor of attempting to create sedition and insurrection among the people of Franklin. After reminding the people that North Carolina had "invited" the West to separate from the East, he admonished the citizens of Franklin to be obedient to the laws of the State of Franklin.[42]

Despite the manifesto, it appeared that the State of Franklin might continue to exist, and Campbell stepped up his campaign to join it. He continued attacking Virginia's tax laws and urged that Washington County send no representative to the General

Assembly. On one occasion he told a group of Southwest Virginians they had paid "two million of money over and above" what was due the government, and urged them to pay no more taxes. He was interrupted by his antagonist, William Russell, who charged that Campbell's information was wrong and designed to mislead the people in order to set them against the government. Russell told the group they could pay their taxes by selling their cattle. Some responded to this suggestion by vowing to take up arms before paying any more taxes. Campbell praised this stand stating "he liked men who would take up arms before paying so unjust a tax." The meeting broke up amidst hurrahs for liberty.[43]

This scene was repeated at meetings throughout the county. Campbell's chief opponent continued to be William Russell who reminded the people that going along with Campbell and refusing to pay taxes could result in rebellion. In such a case, he pointed out, Virginia would be assisted by the United States government. Campbell replied that "they need not be alarmed, that we could obtain, at any time, sufficient assistance."[44]

In order to succeed, Campbell and the other new state makers needed the support of Congress. For this purpose, a petition from the separatists along with a set of resolutions under the title "Association" was sent to the president of Congress. The petition was read to that body on January 13, 1785. It expressed the elation of the western inhabitants over the resolves of Congress respecting the western territory. The people on the frontier hoped they might "speedily enjoy the advantages of such a government as will be exercised over a convenient territory, not too small for the support of authority nor too large for the security of freedom."

> That our situation is such, inhabiting valleys intermixed with and environed by vast wilds of barren and inaccessible mountains, that the same compensation of latitude alotted to the new States northwest of the Ohio might prevent us from ever being on an equal footing with our neighbors, blessed with so many natural advantages, navigable Waters, and a level, fertile Country.
>
> That a State bounded by a meridian line that will touch the confluence of Little River near Ingles Ferry, thence down the Kanhawa to the Ronceverte or Green Briar River, thence Southwest to Latitude 37° north, thence along the same to the meridian of

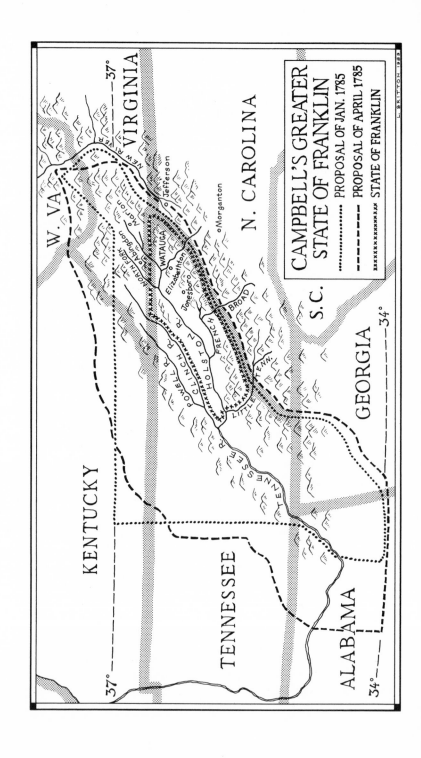

CAMPBELL'S GREATER
STATE OF FRANKLIN

PROPOSAL OF JAN. 1785 ....
PROPOSAL OF APRIL 1785 — — —
STATE OF FRANKLIN xxxxxxxxxxxxx

L. BRITTON 1989

the Rapids of the Ohio, south along the meridian until it reaches the Tenesee or Cherokee river, down the same to the part nearest latitude 34° South to the same, and eastwardly on that parallel to the top of the Apalachian Mountains, and along the highest parts of the Same, and the heights that divide the Sources of the waters that fall into the Mississippi from those that empty into the Atlantic to the Beginning. This, tho' not equal in quantity of habitable lands with the adjoining States, yet may be sufficient territory for a society that wishes to encourage industry and temperance as cardinal virtues.

That in our present settlements we have maintained our ground during the late perilous War, and frequently gave effectual aid to our Brethern to the South and Eastward; that we are first occupants and aborigines of this Country, freemen claiming natural Rights, and the privileges of American Citizens.

Our pray'r, therefore, is, that your Honourable Body, with a generous Regard to the Rights of mankind, would speedily erect the aforesaid described Territory into a free and Independent State, subject to the foederal Bond, and likewise confirm and guarantee to its Inhabitants all their equitable Rights and Priviledges acquired under the Laws of the States lately claiming this territory; that the disposition of the vacant lands be under the power of the Legislature of the new State, in as full manner as that exercised by such of the Eastern States having unappropriated Lands, with this Reservation, that the monies arizing from the sale of vacant Lands shall be faithfully paid to the order of Congress, towards the payment of the National Debt.[45]

As Frederick Jackson Turner noted, "they desired to erect the upper courses of the Tennessee and the territory about Cumberland Gap into a separate state, a greater Franklin."[46] Actually, Campbell called his proposed state "Frankland," meaning land of freedom, a state which included parts of Southwest Virginia, West Virginia, North Carolina, Georgia, Tennessee, Alabama and Kentucky.[47]

A second petition was drawn up by Campbell and others on April 7, and sent to Congress in the spring of 1785, proposing a modification of Jefferson's ordinance of 1784 to allow the creation of two states with natural boundaries—Kentucky, bounded by the Great Kanawah, to make one, and the upper waters of the Tennessee, including Muscle Shoals, the other. The petitioners reinforced their appeal by pointing out how their blood was spilled in acquiring land for their settlements. Their fortunes were expended in making the frontier habitable and they asserted "for ourselves we fought, for ourselves we conquered, and for ourselves alone have we a right to hold" the land.[48] Although many members of Congress supported them, the petitioners failed to get sufficient support for their scheme, and by now, Patrick Henry, governor of Virginia, was becoming increasingly alarmed at the activities of the malcontents in the West. The Virginia Assembly passed an act for reorganizing the county militias and for "guarding against invasion and insurrections." The act gave the governor and council the authority to replace field officers, including county lieutenants. It was to go into effect on April 1, 1785, although Article XIII provided for the suspension of the act in the western counties as long as the governor and council thought proper. The governor suspended the operation of the act until January, 1786, after being advised to do so by the council. The delay was probably because of a threat of renewed Indian hostility on the frontier.[49]

By June, 1785, Campbell's activities induced the council to inform the governor that it had "good reason to believe that the present county lieutenant of Washington, and some other persons . . . are endeavoring to alienate the affections of the people there from this Commonwealth." The council advised the governor to put the militia act into operation in Washington County, which Henry did by issuing a special proclamation.[50] The field officers of the Washington County militia, who were active in the separatist movement, were removed and replaced with friends of the government. Campbell was removed from the office of county lieutenant and replaced by William Russell. Henry's actions were not popular with the majority of the people of the county, since many of those removed were among the most important men in the county, heroes of Kings Mountain and men who had protected the frontier settlements from Indian attacks. Nor did the attempted enforcement of the law have the effect Henry hoped it would.

Sevier, aware of the opposition of Virginia authorities to Campbell's proposed greater State of Franklin, and not wanting to antagonize Patrick Henry, wrote the governor in July:

> Although we have been forced into measures for separating from Carolina, I think it necessary to inform you that we will on no

account, Encourage any part of the people of your state to join us, nor will we receive any of them unless by consent of your state. We reverence the Virginians and I am confident the Legislature here will at all times, do everything to merit their esteem.[51]

At the July term of the Washington County Court, the governor's proclamation was read. Russell, with the rank of general, and his field officers, asked the court to swear them into office in accordance with the law. Ironically, Arthur Campbell was the presiding justice of the court, and he demanded to know by whose authority they sought to hold office. Russell handed Campbell the governor's proclamation but Campbell refused to swear them in. Instead, Campbell left the bench and addressed the court, stating that "he would not tamely submit to it." He stated that "the militia law was tyrannical and oppressive, and recommended to all present to pay no regard to it." According to Campbell the governor and council had exceeded their powers because the governor had suspended the law until January, 1786, and did not have the power to enforce it at this time. "The power of enforcing the law or not," argued Campbell, "was in the Court and not in the Executive, [and] the governor's proclamation was no law."[52]

Russell told the court that if it supported Campbell rather than the governor and council, he would inform the governor. Campbell responded, asking "what was the governor and council? They were no more than an individual ... of the state." Campbell won his point and the court postponed swearing-in the officers until the matter could be discussed with the governor.[53] In addition to the action of the court, some of the leading citizens of Washington County petitioned the governor and council, requesting that the Militia Act not be enforced.[54]

In his proclamation enforcing the Militia Act, the governor had specifically named Campbell as a leader of the separatists and on July 26, 1785, Campbell wrote Henry in defense of his position. He told the governor that the westerners had expected a redress of their grievances by Congress and the Legislature but this had not occurred. "We are told ... that we have offended government on account of our sentiments being favourable to a new state, and our looking forward for a separation," he wrote.

If such a disposition is criminal, I confess there is not a few in this
County to whom guilt may be imputed, and to many respectable
characters in other counties on the western waters. If we wish for
a separation it is on account of grievances that daily become more
and more intolerable.... Why may we not take courage and say
we are right when adverting to our own Constitution, to the
different acts of Congress, that of different legislatures, the opinions of the first statesmen in America, among whom we can number an illustrious commander, a great lawyer, and judge in this
state, and a governor of Virginia himself.[55]

On July 27, 1785, James Montgomery, William Edmiston and
Arthur Bowen sent the governor and council an account of Camp-
bell's activities during the past two years, including his opposition
to the governor's proclamation at the July term of the Washington
County Court. The charges, they said, could be supported by
General Russell, Captain Andrew Kincanon, Captain William
Cocke and Captain Henry Smith.[56]

Henry was forced to take stronger measures and when the October session of the General Assembly convened he informed the
assembly of Washington County's petitions to Congress requesting
a separate state and Campbell's involvement in the matter. The
governor noted that the state proposed by the leaders of the movement, "especially Col. Arthur Campbell," included a vast area of
territory which formed an "invaluable barrier between this country
and those who ... may occupy the vast places westward of the
mountains...."

In addition, this region contained the most respectable militia
Virginia had. If the separatist movement were successful, Virginia
would "lose that barrier for which our people have long and often
fought; that nursery of soldiers, from which future armies may be
levied, and through which it will be almost impossible for our
enemies to penetrate." Henry requested that in dealing with the
issue, the Legislature be lenient, in order to "reclaim our erring
citizens."[57]

The General Assembly fully recognized the gravity of the situation and responded to the governor's message both wisely and
forcefully. The first act passed in the October session reinstated
Campbell to the office of county lieutenant. The other officers

removed under the Militia Act of 1784 were also reinstated.[58] But if anyone had doubts as to where the assembly stood on the separate state movement, they quickly vanished with the passage on the same day of a bill entitled "An Act Punishing Certain Offenses, and Vesting the Governor with Certain Powers." In language that could not be misinterpreted, paragraph II of the popularly-called "Treason Act" stated that:

> Every person or persons who shall erect or establish, or cause and procure to be erected or established, any government separate from or independent of the government of Virginia, within the limits thereof, unless by act of the legislature of this commonwealth . . . [or] those who resist or oppose the due execution of the laws of this commonwealth; shall be proceeded against and punished in the same manner as other traitors may be proceeded against and punished by the laws now in force.

Paragraph IV gave the governor and council the authority to call up the militia to enforce the law.[59]

The Treason Act virtually ended Campbell's efforts to establish the State of Frankland, intended to be a greater State of Franklin. However, the Assembly was realistic enough to see the necessity of some division of Virginia's territory, passing an act which specified the conditions upon which the district of Kentucky could be formed into a separate state.[60] The Kentucky bill must have given Campbell a great deal of satisfaction for he had also been active in the separate state movement in Kentucky. Although Campbell gave up the idea of separating Southwest Virginia, he continued to be interested in separate statehood for Kentucky.[61]

Concerning some of the acts passed by the October session of the legislature, Campbell wrote a close friend that it gave him "no small pleasure to find so many of the bills . . . ," in the process of being adopted. "These with some other advances toward right legislation," he wrote, "induced a wish that I could for aye remain a member of so enlightened a community." But the Treason Act was a different matter. Concerning this bill, he confessed his great astonishment. He had been told that the measure was pushed through at the last minute without giving the legislators an opportunity to study it, but he was hopeful that the Legislature would correct this error in the future.[62]

Campbell was now forced to turn his attention toward maintaining his position of leadership in Washington County. His activities in the new state movement had created many bitter enemies for him, among whom were some of Southwest Virginia's leading citizens. He had incurred the wrath of Joseph Martin when he told the governor of Virginia that Martin had become one of the State of Franklin's privy counselors.[63] Martin flatly denied the statement and made certain he kept aloof from the state makers.[64] This episode caused bad feelings between the Campbell and Martin families that continued for years after the two men passed from the scene.[65]

The most dangerous enemies of Campbell were William Russell, William Edmiston, James Montgomery and others who made up the Russell group. This group utterly detested Arthur Campbell. The issue was no longer the separate state movement, but who would control Washington County politics, the Campbell group or the Russell group. Personal grudges as well as public differences caused the conflict to be even more bitter.

Henry was slow to act on the charge of malconduct made against Campbell in July, 1785, and the following November William Edmiston and four others filed additional charges against Campbell. Believing that the governor would not allow "such atrocious insult to the Commonwealth of Virginia to pass unnoticed" and so that Campbell's "wicked and persevering conduct" could more clearly be understood, they described in detail Campbell's opposition to the Militia Act at the July term of the Court.[66]

In December, James Montgomery officially charged Campbell with malpractices and misconduct in office as a justice of the peace in that:

> 1st. He advised persons chargeable with public taxes to refuse payment thereof.
> 2ndly. That he advised free holders against electing members to the General Assembly—and
> 3rdly. That he attempted by various means, openly and secretly, to induce the inhabitants of Washington County to separate from the Commonwealth.[67]

After considering these and previous charges against Campbell, the Virginia Council, under the authority of the Treason Act, set the first Monday in April, 1786, for considering the evidence. The Council ordered that a copy of the charges be given to Campbell and that between February 1 and March 15, each side was to collect evidence in their behalf. Witnesses were to be given ten days' notice of the time and place they were to be questioned and their testimonies were to be transmitted to the governor.[68]

Witnesses for and against Campbell were heard during the appointed time. One of the most telling testimonies against Campbell was given by William Russell.[69] One of Campbell's strongest defenders was Robert Craig, a captain in the militia. Craig testified that when Campbell stepped from the bench and addressed the court concerning the militia bill, he acted as a "private citizen," and that he only asked the court to delay swearing-in the officers until some misunderstanding could be cleared up between the old officers and the governor. Craig stated that Campbell wanted to leave the choice of enforcing the militia bill to the people, and if they wanted new officers, Campbell would agree to it and "could shoulder his musket as well as any of them...."[70]

Campbell did not attend the hearing in Richmond on April 3, the day appointed by the Council. He cited health and bad weather as excuses.[71] Two days later Campbell and his two attorneys, James Innes and Archibald Stuart, appeared before the board of inquiry. Upon a reading of the charges, Campbell's attorneys objected to the jurisdiction of the board on the grounds that the act under which they were acting (the Treason Act) was contrary to the Bill of Rights, and the principles of the Constitution. This argument was rejected by the board. Campbell's counsel then objected to the way the evidence against Campbell was collected, maintaining that witnesses should appear in person before the accused and that the evidence was acquired in a partial manner.[72]

The board decided that the evidence against Campbell was insufficient because the certificate of the justices attached to the testimonies did not indicate the place as well as the time where the testimonies were taken. The board ordered that new hearings be conducted, this time specifying the Courthouse of Washington County as the place for the hearings. The testimonies taken at these hearings were to be transmitted to the governor no later than the second Tuesday in June, and the parties concerned were to meet in the Council Chamber on that day.[73]

Campbell did everything he could to obstruct the hearings at the Washington County Courthouse. The commissioners appointed to conduct the hearings notified him of the days on which witnesses would be questioned, and requested he be present, but he found reasons to avoid attending. One day he sent his brother, John, to inform the commissioners that he was unable to attend because "he was backward in his spring crops, had whooping-cough in his family, and . . . the notice [sent him] was illegal." On another day Campbell appeared late and succeeded in getting the hearings postponed after arguing that the notice given him was illegal because it did not contain the names of the witnesses against him. Despite Campbell's efforts to disrupt them, the hearings were conducted throughout the month of May, and on June 2, the commissioners reported to the governor they hoped the evidence collected, together with Campbell's own letters in possession of the board, would be sufficient to support the charges against him.[74]

After a series of delays the board of inquiry finally took up the case August 31, 1786. Upon consideration of the evidence for and against Campbell, the five man board, with Spencer Roane dissenting, found him "guilty of misconduct" and recommended his removal from the office of justice of the peace.[75] Henry quickly carried out the recommendation of the board.

Fortunately for Campbell, Henry's term in office soon expired and Edmund Randolph became governor of Virginia. On December 22, 1786, Campbell and Robert Craig, both of whom would soon to be elected to the General Assembly, sent Randolph an address from Campbell's regiment congratulating the newly elected governor. Campbell made it a point to assure Randolph that he greatly admired him and was elated over his election.[76] Randolph, "somewhat embarrassed for a suitable reply," sent a note the next day thanking Campbell and Craig for the trouble they had taken in forwarding the address, and for the "very favourable opinion" they had of him.[77] Two months later the Washington County Court petitioned Randolph requesting that Campbell be allowed to resume his duties as a justice of the peace, and that he rescind

Governor Henry's executive order removing Campbell from office.[78]

The Virginia Legislature passed an act in 1787 declaring the Treason Act unconstitutional, for the very reason that Campbell had argued all along, that is, because the Treason Act gave the Executive powers which interfered with those of the Judiciary. The Treason Act, officially entitled "An Act to Extend the Powers of the Governor and Council," was repealed and Campbell was reinstated by the governor, resuming his duties September 15, 1789.[79]

The Campbell group was now in the ascendance. The Russell party, however, did not go down without a fight. In a last-ditch effort, William Edmiston brought a *qui tam* action[80] against Campbell, that was heard by the Virginia Supreme Court of Appeals. Edmiston argued that Campbell resumed office without being qualified since he did not receive a new commission and was, therefore, in violation of the law. The Court ruled in Campbell's favor with the decision that "the Executive cannot remove a justice of the peace from office. He may be removed by the judgment of a superior court of law.[81]

Meanwhile, in North Carolina, the State of Franklin had run into more difficulties. It, nevertheless, continued a precarious existence under the leadership of Governor Sevier until 1788. An opposition party arose, led by John Tipton, who literally hated Sevier. Civil conflict broke out, and almost civil war, with two governments struggling for control, one established under Franklin's Constitution and the other under the authority of North Carolina. Bloody Indian wars raged in Franklin, brought on by the greed of the Franklinites for Cherokee lands. But the most serious blow to the struggling new state was its failure to gain the support of the Confederation Congress.[82]

Governor Martin had warned in his manifesto that North Carolina would "regain her government over the revolted territory or render it not worth possessing." If Martin was serious about what he said, then the election of Sevier's friend and fellow land speculator, Richard Caswell, governor of North Carolina averted civil war. However, Caswell's successor to the governor's chair, Samuel Johnston, was no friend of Sevier and on July 29, 1788, he ordered the arrest of Sevier, who had, among other things, become involved in a questionable scheme concerning a second secessionist movement, this time with Spanish backing. Tiptonites arrested Sevier and took him east to Morganton to be tried for treason. However, the trial never took place and Sevier was allowed to return to his home where, by now, the State of Franklin had come to an end.[83]

It is obvious that North Carolina authorities could not in good conscience punish Sevier and the other Franklinites. Consequently, North Carolina pursued a conciliatory policy. The former Franklinites, now North Carolinians again, took an oath of allegiance, and many of the separatist leaders soon attained prestigious positions in the state. Sevier was elected to the North Carolina Senate and to the Congress of the United States after the Federal Constitution was ratified. When in 1796, the western North Carolinians finally did get their separate state, this time called Tennessee, Sevier became its first governor.[84]

During the beginning stages of the new state movements, Campbell wrote Arthur Lee: "some considered that I was aiming at public good, others private aggrandizement...." Regardless of what the public thought, he was guided, he said "by two political landmarks: the Consitution and the voice of the people...."[85] In referring to "the Constitution," Campbell probably meant the resolutions of Congress concerning the admission of new states into the Union. A few years later he wrote his friend Archibald Stuart a letter which helps to explain his persistence in what appears to have been a hopeless cause from the beginning. It also casts additional light on why Patrick Henry hesitated in putting an end to the movement. "The truth is...," wrote Campbell, "I pay perhaps too implicit a deference to the acts of the Continental Council. Besides Mr. Henry first suggested to me ideas [and] Col. Christian fostered them, but they can turn and veer, which I cannot when I think I am right...."[86] There is no better evidence that the majority of the people of Washington County also thought he was right than the fact that they overwhelmingly elected Campbell and his main defender, Robert Craig, to the General Assembly in 1787.[87]

Campbell, like the people he represented, took the philosophy of the Declaration of Independence literally, particularly the part which states that governments are instituted among men, deriving their just powers from the consent of the governed; that, whenever any form of government becomes destructive of these ends, it is the right of the people to alter or abolish it, and to institute a new government.

Campbell's greater State of Franklin, or Frankland, was an attempt to put this philosophy into practice. To the back country people, this was what the War for Independence had been all about.

7 Nationalist

The Articles of Confederation (1781–1789) were, according to historian Merrill Jensen, "a constitutional expression of the philosophy of the Declaration of Independence."[1] The articles provided that each state retain its sovereignty, and this seemed to be exactly what most Americans wanted at the time. From experience they knew the dangers of a powerful central government. But the articles proved to be too weak to provide for the needs of the new nation. The articles gave no power to the Confederation Congress to tax the states or regulate commerce. The Congress had no coercieve power over the people or the state governments, resulting in economic chaos, threats of secession and even outright rebellion. Nor could Congress pay its debts, or settle disputes it had with England and Spain.

Some Americans, among them George Washington, Alexander Hamilton and James Madison, recognized that for the nation to survive, the powers of the central government must be greatly strengthened. Between May 25 and September 17, 1787, delegates from the states met in Philadelphia for the historic Federal Convention. The articles were discarded and replaced with the constitution of the United States. This constitution did what the "Nationalists" hoped it would do: greatly strengthened the national government. The founders were fully aware that not all Americans would approve of their work; thus they provided in Article VII of the Constitution that when nine of the 13 states ratified the document by state conventions, the constitution would be put into operation.

The debate between the supporters of the constitution, the Federalists, and the Antifederalists was soon underway.

The Virginia Assembly passed a series of resolutions on October 25, 1787, providing for a convention to accept or reject the constitution adopted by the Federal Convention at Philadelphia. Elections for delegates to the convention were to be held in March, 1788.[2] Arthur Campbell and his party favored the ratification of the constitution but the people of Washington County chose James Montgomery and Samuel Edmundson, who opposed the constitution, to represent them.[3]

The Virginia Convention met June 2, 1788, and debated the constitution until June 27, when it was ratified by a vote of 89 to 79. The opposition was led by Patrick Henry and George Mason. Campbell believed that Henry's opposition stemmed from his personal political ambition. He maintained that Henry was "intoxicated with a love of local power, for although he had ambition, he did not judge he had interest to become chief of the Nation or he would have been a Federalist too...." Campbell attributed the opposition of "the more enlightened Mason" to his excessive love of money and land. "Could he have seen a certainty under the general government to secure his, *Head Rights* and other large grants...," opined Campbell, Mason would also have supported the constitution.[4]

If Arthur Campbell had attended the Virginia Convention he would have voted to accept the constitution. From the very beginning of the new nation he was an ardent supporter of the national government. He never showed the apprehension that the central government might acquire too much power.[5] This might appear puzzling since Campbell was also the champion of local democracy. He believed, however, that democracy and individual liberty would best be insured by the national rather than the state government. It was "the national cement," he said, "from whence all our consequence and safety must flow...."[6] Soon after his marriage, just prior to the revolution, Campbell became inbibed with the "notion that ... [his] views and actions ought to tend to the good of posterity." This idea, he said, "frequently influenced [his] conduct and by the year 1788 had a powerful stimulus...." His "greatest dread" was to be "replunged under a detestable tyranny." He was also greatly concerned that the United States might break up into 13 sovereign states, which would "eventually produce anarchy." He felt that it was better "to have an imperfect Federal Constitution than none, for all human systems will be imperfect." Thus he "embarked heartily in having the Constitution of 1787 adopted."[7]

When George Washington was elected president of the United States, and the new government went into operation, Campbell wrote Archibald Stuart expressing his feelings. "We may not be charged with exaggeration," wrote Campbell, "if we consider . . . [the creation of the Constitution] an event equally friendly to liberty as the Revolution from the domination of Great Britain. . . ." If the government under the Constitution was to operate as it should there must be reciprocal duties between the governor and governed. "The people ought to remember, it ought to be deeply impressed on their minds," he wrote, "that they may have something else to do than barely to elect . . . [representatives]." If the governed were to carry out their responsibilities "regular information ought to be had, ought to earnestly [be] sought after, in order to judge aright, to praise or blame judiciously. An intelligent honest Representative will be pleased to serve such a people. The ignorant and knavish ought to be detected and expelled." How could the people accomplish this? Campbell believed that some of the people were better able to understand the operations of the government than others, but there was a way the people could be advised. He proposed that

> (1) A county library be formed of modern and the most useful books; besides, let each company have at least one newspaper or one of the Congressional Registers.
> (2) Let one, two, or three particular persons in each county be chosen to correspond with the Representative of the district in Congress. This might be called a committee of correspondence.
> (3) Another or the same committee, might be elected to correspond with the committee of other counties.
> This plan with some maturing and additions might have this with other salutory effects. That the Representative might know the sense of his Constituents on the important acts of their passage and before they become a law. This would give him greater confidence, and might suggest some useful hints. In short, it would literally be binding the people by laws made with their own

consent.... It would be productive of a genuine republican spirit, it would tend to unite the American people and make them a band of brothers.[8]

As for the site of the permanent seat of government, Campbell wanted a central location where prices were reasonable to enable representatives to live frugally. But he feared the introduction of European vices, customs and manners if the capital city became a commercial center. This, he said, would alarm him "more for the fate of republicanism than a confederacy of all the Indian tribes against us...." He was also concerned that the Northern states might gain a preponderance of knowledge, property and power, while "we to the Southward with our Blacks and Mongrels, will be the peasantry of the Empire, before half a century." One way to avert this calamity was to abolish slavery or send the blacks out of the country, which he advocated as early as 1782.[9] Campbell continued to oppose the institution of slavery, not only because he felt that it would hold back progress in the South, but also because he believed it was morally evil. After discussing these views with his friend, Samuel McDowell of Kentucky, McDowell responded giving his own view on the subject, and revealing the attitude of many Americans toward the institution of slavery.

> Your remarks about the unhappy people we have as property, I acknowledge to have force, and I fear what may be the consequence one day. But I hope some scheme may be adopted to rid the country of that kind of property. Say if all the females born after a certain time to be free at 18 or 20 years of age and their masters to learn them to spin and sew and to read in the Bible. Their offspring would be free of course.... By this slow method ... slavery would [eventually] be totally gone.... But this is only speculation and I fear no plan will be fallen upon for some time, as lands are much wanted to open this woody country, and my dear Sir, I fear it would be hard to prove from Scripture or the practice of all nations, that slavery is wrong as is a moral evil. We find that Paul was in communion with both master and servant at the same time. But you will say those were hired servants. I say they were not, for whenever the word servant occurs in Scripture I am told it ought to have been rendered slave....[10]

Antislavery feelings were strong in the West after the establishment of the government under the constitution, and in 1795 many of the inhabitants of Washington County freed their slaves. This was the reverse of what was taking place in most of the South for with the invention of the cotton gin in 1793 the fate of black Americans was sealed. Campbell's apprehension for the future of the South proved to be justified.

The great expectation with which Campbell viewed the new government received its first blow, in his estimation, with the passage of Alexander Hamilton's funding program in 1790. The plan was intended to establish the credit of the United States, but to many, including Campbell, it appeared to reward Northern speculators at the expense of the people.

The constitution provided that there would be no nobles or permanent distinction among the people but Campbell believed that the funding system produced the "realities of distinction." It was "the greatest evil, the vortex that will swallow up all, or bring on direful convulsions, and if continued, eventually in the total loss of liberty." Like his fellow Virginian James Madison, a leader in the House of Representatives, he would have "paid those and only those to whom we were indebted for bona fide services rendered, the full amount."[11]

Regardless of some misgivings, Campbell believed, as did the great majority of the people of the United States, that no matter what faults the government might have the nation was safe as long as it was under the leadership of George Washington. Hardly had the president arrived in New York to assume the duties of his office when Campbell wrote him that he was among the president's earlier admirers and offered to advise Washington on problems related to the West.[12]

Washington was genuinely appreciative and replied that the information which Campbell communicated "claims my thanks, and the personal kindness they express is entitled to my great acknowledgements." The president accepted "with pleasure ... [Campbell's] obliging offer to further communications," and told him that he would at "all times be happy to receive such information as ... [Campbell might] think interesting to the Government of the United States."[13]

Henry Knox, the secretary of war, soon wrote Campbell to obtain detailed information on the Southwest.

The public, Sir, are obliged by your attention to the subject of [Indian affairs]. . . . I shall also be obliged by precise answers to the following queries

1. If [Alexander] McGillivary [a half-breed chief of the Creeks] has sent messages to the [Indians] of other nations to find out the exact purport thereof and the answers of the Cherokees thereto

2. If war should ensue with the Creeks what side would the Cherokees take as a nation, would they join them against the United States? Or whether any or what part of the Cherokees would join the arms of the United States.

3. What is the distance of the nearest settlements of Holston to the Cherokee towns, particularly Chota? Have the Cherokees returned to that town?

4. What kind of navigation is it for boats, and the depth and rapidity of the water from Holston and Chota town, the Tennessee to the Muscle Shoals and what is the distance?

5. What is the distance from the Holston settlements to Miro and Nashville settlements on the Cumberland River?

6. The distance from Nashville and Miro settlements to the Muscle Shoals?

7. What nation of Indians are they who commit depredations on the said settlements? What are the number of settlements at Nashville and Miro, and the Cumberland River generally?

8. What is the distance from Lexington in Kentucky to the nearest upper Creek towns. . . .[14]

The Indian problem continued to be of major concern for the state and national governments. Peace between the Cherokee Nation and the United States had been agreed to at the Treaty of Hopewell in 1785. Under the provisions of the treaty Congress was to regulate the Indian trade and no whites were to settle on Indian lands. White settlers paid no attention to the treaty and continued their push into the Indian country. Congress made a feeble effort to stop this, issuing a proclamation in September, 1788, forbidding the instrusion of whites beyond the boundary line.[15] Angered by the failure of the whites to abide by the treaty, the Indians kept the settlements of the southwest frontier in a constant state of fear. Isolated incidents of murder by red men and whites, the treacherous murder of Chief Old Tassel while under a flag of truce, and Spanish influence over the Indians made real peace impossible.[16]

Another effort was made to end Indian hostilities with the signing of the Treaty of Holston in 1791. This treaty was similar to that of Hopewell, with new boundary lines drawn at the expense of the Indians.[17] Once again, violations of the treaty kept the frontier in a state of war.

Throughout these years of conflict, Campbell, as commander of the 70th Regiment, was responsible for the safety of the people of Washington and Russell counties, the latter formed from Washington in 1786. In carrying out his responsibilities he frequently communicated with the governors of Virginia and the president of the United States, requesting aid and making suggestions on how best to deal with the Indians. There is no doubt that his communications influenced the policies of both the state and national governments.

On December 31, 1787, Campbell wrote Governor Edmund Randolph, seeking his aid in securing from Congress an appointment to the office of superintendent of Indian affairs. He told Randolph that whether he was appointed or not, his candidacy would at least create some competition for the post. He cited as his special qualification the knowledge he acquired of the Indian language, customs, and manners while a prisoner of the Wyandottes in his youth.[18] He also wrote a member of the Confederation Congress that his knowledge on Indian affairs was "equal to any man in the Southern states. Nothing . . . could have induced me to offer for so perilous and unprofitable an undertaking considering the deranged state of the District," wrote Campbell, "but a hope that I might be useful at this peculiar crisis of American affairs, to promote peace and security to the Western people and facilitate the adoption of federal measures."[19]

Campbell was greatly disappointed when he was passed over for Joseph Martin, perhaps because of his involvement with the State of Franklin and the fact that he was a controversial figure. However, this did not lessen his concern for the security of the frontier settlements. Campbell believed that the Indians should be made to feel the inconvenience of warfare just as the whites were experiencing it. He told the governor that companies of regular troops should be stationed where they could intercept Indian parties on their way to the settlements or as they returned to their villages with booty. If the former was successful the whites would never suffer the agony of war. If the latter was accomplished the motive of profit from the sale of booty would be removed.[20]

The Indian problem was intensified because of Spanish influence over them. Since the end of the Revolution the issues of free
navigation of the Mississippi River and the Florida boundary line
had been obstacles to good relations between the United States and
Spain. The Spanish government operated on the assumption that
if the American government was unable to protect its western people from Indian attacks and could not gain rights on the Mississippi, the back country would join the Spanish provinces. To accomplish this Spain encouraged the Indians to attack the frontiers
of Georgia, the Carolinas and Virginia. The Creek chief Alexander
McGillivary was one of Spain's most useful agents in arousing the
Indians against the Americans. McGillivary hoped to unite the
Southern Indians and halt the advance of the white men. At
McGillivary's instigation, the Creeks commenced hostilities against
the whites. When Campbell learned that a party of Creeks was
headed for the Holston settlements, he sent one of the Cherokee
chiefs a message in an effort to discourage the Nation from joining
the war party.

> Brother..., listen attentively; ever since the year 1781, when your
> towns were all destroyed for joining the English, the Virginians
> buried the tomahawk deep, and never wish to raise it again against
> their brothers, the Cherokees, but are willing to live in friendship
> as long as the moon endures. It will be your fault if the friendship
> is broken. I venture to promise further, that none of the Virginians
> living on this side of the Cumberland mountains will molest the
> Cherokees without first obtaining orders from our Governor, who
> is a good man, and will see that you have justice done if you remain
> peaceable. He will also call the Kentuckians to account, if they
> have been guilty of destroying any of the friendly Cherokees.
> Brother, call a Council of your head men, give them this Talk,
> exhort them to live peaceable, and wait until the Governor of
> Virginia can hear all the truth, and if his people are to blame, he
> will give ... satisfaction and put a stop to former wrongs; but if
> you rashly go to war and kill innocent people, there may be a great
> deal of blood shed, for we can send a great army against you that
> may destroy you altogether.
> Listen well, You must see that I have now given you good advice
> both for you and your nation. Send me in return an answer, a very
> long talk. Tell me all there is in your heart. If you are for keeping
> the chain of friendship bright, I will be your friend as heretofore,

and do you all the good I can. It will give me pleasure to use means to heal the wounds and dry up the tears of those that have lost their friends, and be strong in endeavors to do justice to all the red people that keep the peace and love the Americans.[21]

Efforts to prevent the Cherokees from joining the Creeks were for the most part successful, but in September, 1792, John Watts,[22] the main chief of the Chickamaugas after the death of Dragging Canoe, set out with a party of Cherokees and Creeks to attack the Holston and Powell's Valley settlements. The war party totalled 281 warriors, 167 of which were Cherokees, 84 Creeks, and 30 Shawnee. Watts planned to strike first at Nashville and then move to Powell's Valley. Just outside Nashville the Indians, over Watts' objections, attacked Buchanan's Fort, which contained 15 white men and a few women. The sharpshooters in the fort were able to repel the attackers and when the fighting was over none of the whites had been killed. The Indians, on the other hand, received heavy losses. Fifteen warriors, including the Creek Chief Talotiskee were killed, and Watts was seriously wounded.[23]

The people of Powell's Valley were thoroughly alarmed and Campbell went in person to Richmond to impress upon the governor the critical state of affairs on the frontier. The Cherokees were not the only Indians to fear, he told the governor, since the Spaniards were urging the Creeks to make war. He asked the governor for authority to call out a company of rangers for three months' service at or near Cumberland Gap, pointing out that it would "be peculiarly mortifying if the frontier of Virginia [were] ... neglected...."[24] The governor consented and the militia was called out, but there was no major action at that time. Watts was discouraged after his defeat at Buchanan's Fort. Fearing a retaliatory expedition to revenge the attack on the Fort, Watts asked the governor of North Carolina for peace. This peace overture was merely a delaying tactic and fighting continued in the Tennessee territory but Watts ceased to be a threat to Southwest Virginia.[25]

One of the problems Campbell encountered in defending the frontier resulted from a boundary dispute between Virginia and North Carolina. The problem was that citizens of Virginia and North Carolina had settled farther west than the boundary line had been drawn, making it difficult for Campbell to draft men for the militia when they claimed that they were citizens of North Carolina. It will be recalled that a dispute as to the proper line broke out when Campbell contested losing an election in 1777. Dr. Thomas Walker and Daniel Smith were appointed to cooperate with Richard Henderson and James Smith of North Carolina to extend the line. After drawing the line some distance, they began to disagree and ran two lines to the Cumberland Mountains. The southernmost line, the Walker line, was agreed to by the Virginia Assembly in 1783, but North Carolina did not approve it until 1790.[26]

The situation was further complicated when North Carolina ceded its western territory, part of which included the area in dispute. In April of 1790 Congress asserted its authority over the territory between the Henderson line and the Walker line. Virginia challenged the authority of the United States government over this territory. In the spring of 1792 the governor directed Campbell to transmit a copy of a Virginia law of December 7, 1791, asserting the state's authority over the territory, and the governor's proclamation to that effect, to William Blount, governor of the Southwest Territory.[27]

Complying with his orders, Campbell wrote Blount June 6, 1792, that he was instructed to exercise the authority of Virginia in the territory, to Walker's line.[28] Blount replied that he conceived it his duty to extend the jurisdiction of the territorial government to Henderson's line, the governor's proclamation and Virginia law notwithstanding.[29] The resulting problem can clearly be seen from Campbell's communication with the governor of Virginia the following October:

> I was assailed with frequent and loud complaints from the inhabitants between Walker's and Henderson's lines, on account of being harassed with orders from two Jurisdictions. Governor Blount is still persisting in considering them as citizens of the S.W. Territory, when at the same time a large majority declare it to be their desire to be annexed to and under the laws of Virginia.[30]

The issue was not settled for many years and only after prolonged court battles between Virginia and Tennessee.[31]

While Campbell was conducting the defense of the frontier he found himself once again confronted with the charge of misconduct, this time for bribery. On August 17, 1793, Captain Andrew Lewis wrote the governor and enclosed letters from a number of militia men. He endeavored to prove that when Campbell drafted men in Washington County in compliance with the governor's orders, some men paid Campbell from five to eight dollars each to be released from duty. Campbell then supposedly ordered Lieutenant Mathew Willoughby to draft men from the Valley to take their place. Lewis accused Campbell of receiving "between two and three hundred dollars" for this. In addition to his taking money, Lewis complained that Campbell drafted men from Russell County, an exposed part of the frontier, to serve elsewhere, thus placing the Valley in greater danger.[32] Lewis concluded his diatribe by suggesting that Campbell should "never be allowed to serve in any office whatever...."[33]

Campbell responded to the charge by asserting that he could "prove he acted according to the law and in strict conformity to the governor's orders...." He argued that Lewis could not get a single person to swear that he gave Campbell money, if he were present. "The commanding officer of Washington [county] always defys his enemies," Campbell exclaimed, "and can with pleasure invite the strict and impartial enquiry of all good citizens into either his moral, political, or military conduct. Can Capt. Lewis submit to a similar enquiry," he asked?[34] In October he wrote the governor that if the charges made by Lewis were true he deserved greater punishment than removal from office, but insisted that they constituted

a false and malicious libel. I was at some expense, and a good deal of trouble in sending ... [the men] out, because, Sir, you may remember the anxiety I expressed for the safety of the inhabitants they were going to defend, and I would much rather have given them a pound than take a shilling off any of them. To me, it is a wonder how it could enter into the heart of Captain Lewis, that I received between two and three hundred dollars from a few drafts last year, when he well knew that no man, not even himself, who is acknowledged to have some address in making money, that could extort such a sum without being immediately complained of, besides the scarcity of money in this country forbid such attempt.... I would go to the way-side and beg before I would adopt the method Lewis seems so dexterous in pointing out....[35]

Campbell pointed out to his accuser that the practice of recruiting men from Russell County "was begun some months before by yourself. What was justifiable for you to do could hardly be criminal in your subaltern...." Campbell advised Lewis that the law, a past practice, and the governor's order encouraged Lieutenant Willoughby to accept substitutes who were better men than some who were drafted. He again denied receiving money and reprimanded the younger Lewis for making such an accusation.

> The story of my receiving two or three hundred dollars ... from militia men to excuse them from service is so improbable, that I am pursuaded you do not seriously believe it. And how such malice could be cherished in your breast against me, who expected returns of justice and civilty, at least, if not gratitude, is something extraordinary. However, I am happy in having it in my power to prove that I did not, and I can say with truth, such a scheme never entered into my mind. For several years before the county of Washington took place under your father, and the late Col. William Preston, I conducted the defence of the Southwestern frontier disinterestedly. Their letters are my vouches how I conducted myself ... [and now] I can appeal to Henry, Jefferson and other Governors.
>
> You are but a young man yet Sir, and it would have become you on your first outset in military matters to have been more circumspect by being careful to have spoken, wrote, and acted consistently, and in no case suffered yourself to be made the instrument of another man's revenge. If you had, few would have rejoiced more than I, at your military advancements....[36]

The charge was supported by one of Campbell's oldest enemies, Arthur Bowens, who certified that Campbell took ten dollars from one of the men called out to serve.[37] However, he later admitted that "all I mentioned to Capt. Lewis was told as an hearsay, and if Lewis put down words that had a different meaning, it was contrary to my knowledge and direction."[38]

Willoughby, who according to Lewis, was ordered to find substitutes for those who paid to get off, wrote the governor that the charge was false. One man, a John Irons "applied to Colonel

Campbell . . . to find a substitute in his place," wrote Willoughby, "for which I was to give as high as five dollars, but to get him for as little as I could." Willoughby pointed out that others asked him to hire substitutes for them, while some hired substitutes for themselves.[39]

David Young, one of the men who it was said paid Campbell, certified that he neither paid nor promised to pay money to Campbell. He testified that in September a "certain person" came to his house and told him to swear that he paid Campbell money to be excluded from the draft. He was astonished, he said, that anyone thought him "so base as to swear falsely against anyone."[40] Young never disclosed who the "certain person" was.

It was common practice on the frontier for a draftee to hire a substitue to take his tour of duty. In this particular case Campbell and Willoughby helped a few men find substitutes, but they received no personal profit for their trouble. This was neither uncommon nor illegal. A court martial was convened but no proof of a violation of the law by Campbell or Willoughby was found.[41] No action was ever taken by the governor over this unfortunate incident. It appears that the charge was concocted by the enemies of Campbell to discredit him and apparently the governor realized this, for the case was dropped.

While the bribery charge was still hanging over his head, Campbell was commissioned an Indian agent by President Washington.[42] It was fitting that the commission came when it did since it obviously bolstered his spirits. It was also fitting that the president recognized his competence at this time because Campbell's years of public service were coming to an end. Campbell communicated with the president throughout his second administration on matters relating to the frontier. On one occasion Campbell prepared a new map of the Southwest, Kentucky and part of the Northwestern territory. He apparently delivered the map to the president in person.[43]

Continued Indian hostility in the southwest justified Washington's desire to maintain close contact with that area. On April 6, 1794, a party of Cherokees led by a chief called Captain Bench attacked a settlement in Washington County. Bench was especially noted for his cruelty in raids on the frontier during the past year.

In this raid he struck the home of a William Todd Levingston. Mrs. Levingston and her children were alone in the house at the time. The children escaped but Mrs. Levingston was captured and taken across the Clinch and Powell's mountains. A party of 13 white men under the command of Lieutenant Vincent Hobbs, of Lee County was sent in pursuit. Several days later contact was made with the Indian raiding party, at which time Bench was killed and Mrs. Levingston was rescued.[44]

Campbell sent information concerning this attack to the governor along with Bench's scalp. "I now send the scalp of Captain Benge [sic], that noted murderer, as requested by Lieut. Hobbs," he wrote, "as a proof that he is no more...." Campbell described how Hobbs had killed the Indian and suggested that he be rewarded with a "neat rifle," which "would serve as a stimulus for future exertions against the enemy."[45] Following this request the General Assembly voted to send Hobbs a silver mounted rifle.[46] The need for "future exertions," however, was fortunately almost over, as the attack of April 6 has been considered "the last recorded invasion of Southwest Virginia by the red men."[47]

There were several reasons for the end of Indian hostilities in Southwest Virginia at this time. Fighting had broken out between the Cherokees and the Chickasaws, and the death of McGillivary in 1793 ended any hope of uniting the southern Indians against the whites. The increased population of Tennessee served as a barrier between Virginia and the Indian country. The changed attitude of Spain which resulted in Pinckney's Treaty (October 27, 1795) was also a factor. By the terms of this treaty, negotiated by Thomas Pinckney at Madrid, Spain agreed to the right of Americans to deposit their goods at the port of New Orleans, and the Florida boundary dispute was settled. Both counties agreed to restrain hostilities of the Indians living within their territory.

On June 26, 1794, the Cherokees signed a treaty with the United States which provided for "re-establishing peace and friendship." Paragraph II provided for the drawing of recognizable boundary lines. Other provisions included an agreement by the United States to provide supplies annually for the Cherokees to the amount of $5,000 and an agreement by the Cherokees to prevent horse stealing.[48] Major General Anthony Wayne's victory over the northern tribe at Fallen Timbers in Ohio in August, 1794, was an added incentive for the Cherokees to remain peaceful.

With the Indians of the Northwest and Southwest somewhat pacified and as pioneers poured into Kentucky and Tennessee (admitted into the Union as states in 1792 and 1796, respectively), there was an increased demand for more reliable mail delivery. The first post office was established at Abingdon, April 25, 1793, with Gerard T. Conn as postmaster.[49] Prior to this time mail was delivered only when a person could be found who happened to be going in the proper direction. Efforts were soon made to create mail routes throughout the West.

In August, 1794, Campbell wrote Timothy Pickering, the postmaster general, proposing a mail route from Staunton to Abingdon,[50] and several months later he was awarded a contract for this route of approximately 224 miles at $2.50 per mile.[51] Campbell also succeeded about a year later in getting Conn, the postmaster of Abingdon, removed, after convincing the new postmaster general, Joseph Habersham, that Conn was incompetent. Campbell was then authorized to appoint a new postmaster.[52] It was not long, however, before Campbell was himself criticized for similar reasons. He was advised by Habersham that "some of the people from the Southwest Territory say that they derive little or no advantage from the mail, as it is carried so irregularly on your route, as to destroy the necessary confidence in it." He urged Campbell to instruct his rider to "conduct the business committed to their charge in a more satisfactory manner...."[53] Campbell agreed to deal with the matter and then proposed that the old mail route down the Ohio be replaced with a route along the Wilderness Road. After serious consideration the plan was rejected because the weight of the mail would require the express rider to employ an additional horse, making a new route more expensive.[54]

When Postmaster General Habersham rejected his latest proposal, Campbell turned to his friend Joseph Anderson about a new project. Anderson of Tennessee had filled the Senate seat vacated by William Blount in 1797. It had come to Campbell's attention that the United States planned to hold a conference with the Cherokees at Tellico to settle a boundary dispute with Tennessee. Campbell quickly wrote Anderson asking him to use his influence with the secretary of war to get his friend Ebenezer Brooks appointed secretary for the American Commissioners. "I am sure I can procure the approbation of Mr. Washington," which he was certain would be of great value.

What Campbell was really after was a contract to furnish the supplies for the conference. "I am so solicitous for the success of the" peace effort, he wrote, "that if you could provide me with some plausible excuse to attend the Treaty I would readily be present." Campbell suggested that the excuse be a contract to furnish the provisions for the conference. If Anderson agreed, "privacy and reservedness with several members [who could get him the contract] will be proper."[55]

Failing to get either request, he turned to Timothy Pickering, now the secretary of state, to help him and his partners get a contract to supply the troops which were to be stationed on the Mississippi River. As if to apologize for making such a request Campbell added that they did not expect to be awarded the contract on better terms. We "only wish the opportunity to have an equal chance with those that are better acquainted with the secretary of war," wrote Campbell, "and whose near residence to the seat of government gives them an opportunity to be more favorably listened to."[56]

Campbell had reason to expect success from Pickering, who had gotten him his mail contract and also a job with the government for his son-in-law.[57] This time, however, the secretary of state was unable to be of assistance. Campbell, expressing his disappointment after failing to get the contract, wrote Pickering, "I may no longer be in suspense, and I hope the gentlemen whose proposals are preferred will fulfill all the public purposes of the contract equal to anything me and my friends could [do]...."[58]

It would not be difficult to argue that Campbell supported the Federalist Party largely because of his vast land holdings in the West and the patronage he received from President Washington and members of his cabinet. This view appears all the more valid when one considers that he quietly opposed many Federalist policies, including Hamilton's funding program, Jay's Treaty and the Alien and Sedition Acts. However, it must be insisted that Campbell's reasons for supporting the Federalists go much deeper than personal gain.

He was an ardent admirer of presidents Washington[59] and Adams, and continued to support the latter even though he failed on several occasions to obtain desired patronage. He continued to express himself on issues when he saw some threat to national unity or security, including the rise of the Jeffersonian Republicans.

One of the early threats to the stability of the Union which greatly concerned Campbell was the "Blount Conspiracy." There were, however, personal reasons too for his opposition to Blount. When Tennessee sought admission into the Union in 1796, he appealed to Washington to delay it until a new constitution was adopted. Campbell felt that the present constitution of Tennessee was inadequate, largely because of an omission of an article recognizing the authority of the United States over Indian lands.[60] The Campbell party in Tennessee had never been able to gain political control from the Blount and Sevier interests. Consequently Campbell's land speculating activities in Tennessee were drastically curtailed.

Campbell kept a watchful eye on what was going on in the new state and quickly communicated to Timothy Pickering anything that would discredit the party in office. He did not have long to wait, for Blount became involved in a scheme where his frontier followers and Indian allies, with the cooperation of the British fleet, were to attack Spanish Florida and Louisiana in order to transfer control of these provinces to Great Britain. In preparation for this event Blount wrote an interpreter in the Cherokee Nation suggesting that he put the Indians in the right frame of mind. This letter fell into the hands of Pickering in July, 1796, while Blount was in the United States Senate. When Congress learned of the "Blount Conspiracy" it immediately expelled him. The House of Representatives began impeachment proceedings but the Senate dismissed the case in 1799 for lack of jurisdiction.[61]

Campbell, meanwhile, tried unsuccessfully to implicate Sevier and his followers. When news of Blount's involvement in some kind of scheme reached Campbell he at once wrote Pickering that the president might find it interesting to inquire as to what Sevier's connection with Blount was and how many other leading characters of Tennessee showed a disposition to become involved in Blount's enterprise. He suggested that Governor George Matthews of Georgia might be involved, since he was in the state along with a "strange resort of leading men and others from Georgia . . . [who] some say . . . are officers and soldiers. . . ."[62]

Campbell was not sure just what the Blount group was up to, but he sent Pickering a list of names of men who did know. There was talk of recruiting men, he said, and "a few days ago a large quantity of lead was engaged at the Lead Mines in Virginia, for the use of a secret expedition."[63] Campbell advised the secretary of state that if there were not enough regular troops near Knoxville to put down the insurgents, they could be reinforced with a regiment of Virginia militia, obviously under the command of Campbell, who "would show to these desperados that our national government must be respected." He assured Pickering that the "voices of the friends of order, are on your side. . . ."[64]

In a long pro–British letter, August 18, 1797, Pickering answered many of the questions Campbell raised. It was by no means certain what Blount's plans were, but he suggested that the British government would not agree to any scheme which involved the use of Indians or violated the neutral rights of the United States. It was more probable that the French were trying to involve the United States in a war with Great Britain and Spain. "The probability is," Pickering wrote Campbell, "that Blount's real plan was connected with French and Spanish politics, covered with the veil of a British scheme. . . ."[65]

The election of Andrew Jackson and Judge Joseph Anderson over Blount and Cocke in the senatorial race of 1797 was mistakenly interpreted by Campbell as an overthrow of the old regime, but in fact Blount had refused to run and Jackson and Anderson were his friends. According to Campbell this setback, along with the arrival of federal troops under Colonel Thomas Butler, caused most of the men in the state to support the federal government and put an end to Blount's plans in Tennessee. For those who were not willing to support the Union, Campbell would "as freely put on . . . [his] arms to oppose such invaders of our national rights, as . . . [he] would to resist Spain in claiming above the thirty-first degree. . . ," or the northern boundary line of Spanish Florida."[66]

Just as he was alarmed at any internal threat to the security of the nation, so too was Campbell concerned over the country's involvement in a war with France over the XYZ Affair, a French demand for money before negotiating with American diplomats. On foreign affairs, like many domestic policies, Campbell appeared more of a Jeffersonian that a Federalist, but he would never have accepted that label. He was extremely distressed over the likelihood of America going to war with the very nation to which she was so much indebted for her own freedom from tyranny. According to Campbell, the root of the difficulty between the two countries was Jay's Treaty with England. This Treaty was "a Pandora's Box," which accounted for the misunderstanding likely to lead to "bloody war."[67] Increasing anti–French sentiment in the country caused him to write Jefferson expressing his sorrow over what appeared to be the rise of a party which was endeavoring to separate the country from its friendly relations with France. Jefferson agreed with Campbell, but consoled him by pointing out that the pro–English party had reached its peak.[68]

Although he regretted very much the prospect of war with France, Campbell favored a strong stand against such French insults as the "XYZ Affair." He advocated a large army and navy and "would freely part with all [his property] in taxes, rather than the United States ... bow *too low* to any nation on earth."[69] He agreed whole-heartedly with Jefferson who wrote him that "we owe gratitude to France, justice to England, good will to all, and subservience to none."[70]

While he agreed with Jefferson on many matters concerning the nation, like other Federalists, Campbell was apprehensive over the rise of the Jeffersonian Republicans. When he publicly opposed the Republicans he was accused by some of his constituents of changing his republican principles to those of aristocracy and monarchy. Responding to this attack he made public a treatise entitled "A Letter to a Young Man," expressing his philosophy of government. In the letter he "endeavored to show the preference of ... representative government to any [other] in the world and that excessive liberty and equality is as much destructive [to liberty] ... as a monarch." He believed that if the Union was threatened, so too was liberty, for as he said, the principles of republicanism were "union, liberty and independence." Destroy any one of these and "the others will vanish, independence would be instantly lost by disunion, and

liberty, civil and religious would depart with it."[71] He was opposed
to anything that challenged the authority of the Federal Government since he viewed this as a threat to the Union. He was strongly
opposed to the growth of republican societies, and although he
thought that the Alien and Sedition Acts were unwise, he did not
condone the activities of the Kentucky Legislature in passing the
Kentucky Resolutions, strong assertions of states' rights, the compact theory of government, and limited national authority.[72]

Feeling as he did toward the Republicans, Campbell must have
viewed with great apprehension the election of Jefferson to the
presidency in 1800. Perhaps it was more than a coincidence that he
chose to retire from public service about the time the Republicans
came to power. Having publicly supported the Federalist he could
expect nothing in the way of patronage from the Jeffersonians.
When the 70th Regiment of the Virginia militia was reorganized in
1799, Campbell retired.[73] This was the first time since its formation
in 1777 that he was not its commanding officer. It was about this
time that he retired also as presiding justice of the Washington
County Court. Already in his late fifties, Campbell began to fade
from the political scene.

8 The Final Years

Arthur Campbell lived at Royal Oak, the present site of Marion, in Smyth County, for over 30 years. During this time he witnessed the transition of Southwest Virginia from a few scattered families struggling for survival along the Holston River to a prosperous and well established region. Washington County alone had by 1800 a population of 9,156 including 817 slaves.[1] Counties and states had sprung up around him as the pace of the westward movement increased.

Involved as he was in public affairs, Campbell spent much of his time at Royal Oak earning a livelihood from the soil. He was not just a farmer, however, but also an alert businessman with an eye for quick profits. He developed the salt mines on the property of his niece, Sarah Campbell; he owned a flour mill and handled the mail for the county, but his greatest investment was in land. Like others who were in a position to do so, Campbell speculated in land. It will be recalled that his first property was granted to him for his service in the French and Indian War, 1,000 acres of which were located near the Falls of the Ohio River. In 1796, he paid property taxes in Kentucky for this plot in addition to 600 acres in Lincoln County on Yellow Creek, 600 acres on Bucke Creek and 400 acres in Hardin County on the Ohio. He owned 1,965 acres in North Carolina, while in Virginia he possessed 13,817 acres in Lee County and 5,000 acres in Washington County. The number of acres he owned varied from year to year as he was always buying and selling land.[2]

The cultivation of Campbell's land in Washington County was apparently done primarily by his family, which included his wife, six sons and six daughters. He had a few indentured servants at one time,[3] but was strongly opposed to slavery and it appears that he never owned any slaves.[4] Some of his property outside Washington County was looked after by tenants.[5]

Soon after he retired, Campbell went to Kentucky on business concerning his property.[6] Although he returned to the Holston from time to time, he was seldom at Royal Oak after 1800. Around 1809 he moved just across the Virginia line and settled on his 600 acre plot at Yellow Creek near Cumberland Gap.[7] Here on the future site of Middlesboro, Kentucky, he lived the remainder of his life.

Although retired from public life, Campbell did not lose his interest in politics. He was especially concerned over the *Marbury v. Madison* decision, anticipating many dangerous consequences if the Supreme Court determined the constitutionality of acts of Congress. To his nephew, David Campbell, who later became governor of Virginia, he wrote that even if the Court decided only the "very glaring and important cases . . . may we not apprehend the judges . . . may err through ignorance or worse motives." One might argue, he said, that "a judge's knowledge is very extensive and his reasoning powers great. . . ." However, Campbell noted that "human reason is not an infallible guide [and] that the faculty of reason has led men to the most corrupt decisions." He felt that scientific knowledge did not "always guide the mind to a just judgement. . . ." As to whether the court or the legislature should determine how the constitution would be interpreted, Campbell favored the law-makers, but confessed that he saw difficulties either way.[8]

There was very little for Campbell to do now. Most of his business was conducted by his sons, giving him plenty of leisure time to correspond with family and friends. He was especially concerned about his daughter Peggy's education. In June, 1801, he wrote to her

> . . . I hoped to have heard you had improved your hand write, that you had read a lesson or two every day. These are not only embellishments of the female character, but useful and necessary

accomplishments to help you pass on through life with propriety and advantage.[9]

In May, 1803, he again wrote Peggy admonishing her to

amuse yourself with reading some every day of the Newspaper or some new Book. It is from events published in Newspapers, that half the conversation of well bred people is now extracted, besides the moral lessons therein recorded.[10]

In the letters to his daughters, he discussed, in addition to the importance of study, religion, his business situation, the illness of his wife who apparently suffered from severe arthritis, the problems he had with his son, William, and all the other things that a person, who believed their life was nearing an end, would be concerned about.[11] He wrote his son John Campbell with advice on how to be a good lawyer, suggesting that the young man broaden his mind by reading history. "As for history," wrote Campbell,

you can not be too extensively acquainted with it. It is history that develops the human character by displaying the actions of men of all ages, and to know mankind will be much the business of a good [lawyer]. But the main matter in your progress in life is to learn to know yourself. . . .[12]

To David Campbell, who later provided Lyman C. Draper with so much material on the family, Campbell frequently reminisced about the great events that had occurred during his lifetime. Being a military man he naturally dwelled on great battles of the past. Recalling the French and Indian War he wrote: "The history of General [James] Wolfe's labours and heroism, must give an animating turn to the minds of all that have ambition to acquire military fame."[13] But it was the Battle of Kings Mountain that stood out most in Campbell's mind. American histories were being published and he was very dissatisfied with the lack of importance attached to Kings Mountain. He constantly stressed the importance of truth in writing history; and he was furious when he heard that John Randolph had remarked in the House of Representatives that Cowpens was the most important battle fought in the South during the American Revolution. Campbell wrote his nephew:

> Thus you see that errors may be introduced into history, which of all writings ought to have a strict regard to truth. We ought to say rather too little, than too much, in the narrative part; if we indulge in supposition, or hyperbole, let it be in addressing the moral and political tendency of great actions.[14]

It appeared to Campbell that he would have to write his own history of the Revolution if the true story was ever to be known. The commemoration of the Battle of Kings Mountain at Abingdon, October 6, 1810, increased his desire to write about the Revolution and he began to collect material for that purpose.[15]

Campbell's history was never written as he died less than a year after the commemoration at Abingdon. He was in poor health much of the time following his retirement. In 1801 he thought he was "at the gate of death."[16] This may have been related to the long and painful illness of cancer of the face from which he eventually died. Although he believed he was in the best of health the following year, his condition over the next several years grew worse.[17]

In May, 1808, he wrote Peggy,

> Doctor M. Cubbin still gives me hope that the sore on my face will be cured, but he blames me for not observing his directions. The fact is I cannot, for I have to attend the business of the Estate so often, that instead of the sore being dressed every 24 hours, I sometimes have to let it pass three days....[18]

On the morning of August 8, 1811, Campbell's son, Arthur Lee, paid him a visit. Campbell was ill in bed, but his son was not aware of the severity of his condition. At noon Arthur Lee prepared to leave for home and went to his father to say goodbye. Campbell clasped his son's hands with both of his and insisted that he stay, saying that his son "would see the last of him that night." About two hours before dark Arthur Lee and his brother James, who were about a quarter of a mile from the house, were sent for. When they arrived, Campbell was coughing and attempting to expectorate. Arthur Lee sat next to the bed to support his father's head, who still had the strength to raise his hand and speak. He reached out to his daughter Patsy and said farewell and then reached to his daughter Ann, then to his wife, and finally the others, saying farewell to each. At last he exclaimed: "Oh death where is your sting; oh grave where is thy victory." Still he clung to life. Arthur Lee laid down on a bed at the foot of his father. After a short time Mrs. Campbell informed the children that their father was dying. Describing his father's death, Arthur Lee wrote:

> the tears of those around him appeared to create an inclination in him to speak, but he could not. With a serene, composed countenance, he cast an expressive look on those around him and expired without a struggle, and scarcely a moan. He retained the full vigor of his mind to the last and showed how a Christian could die.[19]

In accordance with his wish Campbell was buried at a place called Gideon's Tenements near Cumberland Gap.[20]

The "Last Will and Testament" of Arthur Campbell was read in the Knox County, Kentucky, Court, September 2, 1811. In it he provided for the distribution of about 17,000 acres of land among the members of his family and for the distribution of his stock of horses, cattle, and hogs. Apparently, he had very little currency when he died for when money was required for the execution of the will it was raised by the sale of some of his property. His son Charles was left $500 to complete his education. As opposed as Campbell was to slavery, it is interesting to note that his will provided for a plot of land to be sold to purchase one or two Negro women to attend his wife, and if his daughters requested them they were to be provided Negro girls above the age of ten. To his son William and daughter Elizabeth he left a gold ring and Bible, and to his son James his "survey and compass."[21] This was about all of the tangible effects of Arthur Campbell's life of almost 68 years.

It is of course difficult to evaluate the significance of anyone's life, but there are some aspects of Arthur Campbell's that afford a basis for an interpretation of his contribution to American civilization. In the "Introduction" to *The Conquest of the Old Southwest*, Archibald Henderson wrote:

> The romantic and thrilling story of the southward and westward
> migration of successive waves of transplanted European peoples
> throughout the entire course of the eighteenth century is the his-
> tory of the growth and evolution of American democracy.... A
> series of dissolving views thrown upon the screen, picturing the
> successive episodes in the history of a single family as it wended its
> way southward along the eastern valleys, resolutely repulsed the
> sudden attack the Indians, toiled painfully up the granite slopes of
> the Appalachians, and pitched down into the transmontane wil-
> derness upon the western waters, would give to the spectator a
> vivid conception, in miniature, of the westward movement....[22]

Such a picture is found in the life of Arthur Campbell. He was
born of immigrant parents on the savage frontier of Augusta
County, Virginia, and grew to manhood under the hardships and
dangers of this frontier. At the age of 27, Campbell with a few other
pioneers settled in the wilderness of Southwest Virginia. He was a
leading participant in the "taming of the west" and the establishment of territorial, state, and county governments that always followed the westward migration.

For over a quarter of a century Campbell was the recognized
spokesman of many of the people of the southwest, particularly the
citizens of Washington County, Virginia. During and after the
Revolution he was directly responsible for the safety of the inhabitants of a vast region which included parts of Kentucky, Tennessee and Southwest Virginia. He represented the western people
in the Virginia Assembly at the most crucial times during the Revolution and many times thereafter.

What was it about Arthur Campbell that raised him to prominence in the region where he lived? No doubt family ties and friend-
ships played an important part during the early years, but this alone
could not have sustained him for some 25 extremely difficult years.
The answer is more likely to be found in his character. Much has
been said about Campbell's negative disposition, but this, in the
final analysis, was not important. What was important was that
Campbell was a man of the people who thought, and acted, for the
most part, on their behalf. Campbell was the embodiment of the
frontier individual which Frederick Jackson Turner and others
have done so much to popularize. He was literally big and mean,
even ruthless when he found it necesssary, although he was at times

sensitive and gentle. In various ways he resembled Andrew Jackson, Daniel Boone and Patrick Henry. A description of him by his enemies might easily be mistaken for one of Jackson; his adventures on the frontier were comparable to Boone's; his love of liberty equaled that of Henry. Proud, independent, religious, and patriotic — these were common traits on frontier America and they had to be exaggerated in frontier leaders.

Campbell's part in defending Southwest Virginia during the many years of Indian warfare, his assistance in defending the outposts of Kentucky during the Revolution, his campaigns against Loyalists, and his role in organizing the expedition against Ferguson at Kings Mountain are the most obvious contributions he made to his country. Also important was his influence on the growth of democracy. Campbell was an ardent patriot who took literally the philosophy of the Declaration of Independence. One of the more enlightened and outspoken leaders of the West who demanded equality with the East, he accelerated the development of democracy which has been so much associated with the West.

As significant as his contributions were to the development of the West, Campbell has been all but forgotten. One reason is because he was only one of many men who made the westward movement possible. Some of these men, important as they were in American history, have been ignored by historians who focus their attention on national figures. Another reason is that he lived among giants like Washington, Jefferson, Madison and Henry. Beside these men, Campbell appears to be much less than the man he was. However, it was men like Campbell who helped raise those giants to greatness.

It no longer stands, but in 1815 Arthur Campbell's son Arthur Lee erected at his father's grave a tombstone to perpetuate the memory of his pioneer father. On it were inscribed the following words:

Sacred to the memory of
COLONEL ARTHUR CAMPBELL

Who was born in Augusta County, Va., on Thursday, November 3rd, Old style, 1743, and after a well-spent life, as his last moments did and well could approve, of 67 years, 8 months, and 26 days, ere a constitution preserved by rigid temperance and otherwise moral and healthy, could but with reluctance consent, the lamp was blown out by the devouring effects of a cancer on the 8th day of August, 1811, A.D., leaving a widow, six sons and six daughters to mourn his loss and emulate his virtues.

Here lies entombed a Revolutionary sage,
An ardent patriot of the age,
In erudition great, and useful knowledge to scan,
In philanthropy hospitable, the friend of man.
As a soldier brave, virtue his morality
As a commander prudent, his religion charity,
He practiced temperance to preserve his health,
He used industry to acquire wealth.
He studied physic to avoid disease.
He studied address likewise to please.
He studied himself to complete his plan,
For his greatest study was to study man.
His stature tall, his person portly,
His features handsome, his manner courtly.
Sleep honored Sire in the realms of rest,
In doing justice to thy memory a son is blest,
A son inheriting in full thy name,
One who aspires to all thy fame.[23]

Appendices

A An Address to the Freemen of Washington County, Virginia [ca.1782]

Drawn up by Arthur Campbell and the Other Separatists

Your Deputies, after mature Consideration, have agreed to address you on a subject of your Public affairs, well knowing that there is only wanting an exact and Candid examination into the facts to know whether You have been well served or abused by Your representatives, wither Government has been wisely administered, and wither your rights and Liberties are secure. As members of Civil Society, you will acknowledge that there are duties of importance and lasting obligations which must take place before individual conveniences or private interest, but it must be granted that in free Communities the Laws are only obligatory when made consonant to the Constitution or original Compact; for it is the only means of the surrender then made, the power therein given, that the Right ariseth to Legislate at all. Hence it is evident that the power of Legislators is in nature of trust to form regulations for the Good of the whole, agreeable to the powers deligated and the Deposite put into the General Stock, and the end proposed is to obtain the greatest Degree of happiness and safety, not for the few, but for the many. To attain these ends, and these only, men are induced to give up a portion of their natural Liberty and property when they Enter into Society. From this it is plain rulers may exceed their Trust, may invade the remaining portion of natural liberty and property, which would be an usurpation, a breach of a solemn obligation, and ultimately a conspiracy against the majesty of the People, the only treason that can be committed in a commonwealth. A much admired Writer on the side of Liberty, begins his work with the following remarkable sentence, which we Transcribe for Your information, and intreate you to read and Ponder it well: "In every Human Society there is an effort continually tending to confer on one part the hight of power and Happiness and reduce the other to Extreme weakness and misery. The intent of good laws is to oppose these Efforts, and to defuse their influence universally and equally. But men generally abandon the care of their most important concerns to the uncertain Prudence and Discretion of those whose Interest it is to reject the best and wisest Instructions, and it is not till they have been led into a thousand mistakes in matters the most essential to their Lives and Liberties, and are weary of Suffering, that they can be induced to apply a remedy to the evils with which they are oppressed. It is then they begin to conceive and acknowlege the most Palpable Truths, which from their very Simplicity, commonly escape Vulgar minds, Incapable of analysing objects, accustomed to receive impressions without Discretion, and to be determined rather by opinions of others than by the result of their own Examination.

A few plain Questions you may Honestly put to your selves, when in retirement, or when your heads are reclined on your pillows; For what end hath the Almighty wrought out such a wonderfull revolution in the affairs of Men as that of the Independence of America? What part ought I to act through the remainder part of my life, so as to be most pleasing to my Creator and the most useful to Society? Whether is my head and Heart so enlightened and in such a frame as to Attend to and receive the Truths, whether it comes from a person I dislike or not? Are not the duty we owe the Succeeding Generation equal to that I owe the present? Several mediums of Knowledge are open to all diligent inquirers. The productions of the Printing press, Literly Schools, and the meetings of the people to Debate on Public measures. The Inhabitance of this County have as hitherto been peculiarly circumstanced. They became possessors of a Wilderness at a perilous Era; the Greatest part of their time since have been necessarily employed merely to provide subsistance, Course clothing and cheap Dwellings, to defend their familys from the Inclemency of the weather; no time or money to spare to build Elegant and Convenient houses to erect suitable places for public Worship, to found Seminaries for Classical Learning, to promote the Education of Youth, that most indispensable of all obligations to Children. It's also a prior duty to any you owe the Estate to provide food and raiment of Your families. Plain, fair and course clothing you might be content with if it was necessary to part with all supperfluities to answer the real Exigencies of the State; and did you See your fellows in more favourable Situation pursuing the same course, and also could you be persuaded that a Judicious Economy pervades all the disbursements of all the public money, then, and not till then, ought you freely to part with the produce of Your Industry at the call of rulers. It may be alledged by your enemies that you do not mean to contribute anything to alleviate the burthens of the nation and support government. This charge will vanish on a fair enquiry into the various schemes of Finance and the Present State of the Public funds. . . .

If your Eastern neighbours were generous they would make some allowance for the great losses sustained by the Depredations of the Indians, and for the many valuable lives lost to Keep them safe. The appropriation of your public money ought also to be a subject of serious enquiry. For, if at any time, should it be applied to the purposes Vainality and Corruption, you would then be feeding your destroyers, and enable them to make further invasions on your remaining rights and liberties, until you would have nothing left worth Contending for, and you and your posterity would be obliged to stoop to an abject Vassalage.

All is not lost yet. Therefore beware in future of the Objection of either weak or interested Men, who would persuade you to a passive conduct under all the Measures of Government. Your rulers, as well as those of other nations, are only falable men. When they act well, honour and applaud; then wickedly, impeach and punish them. Disregard their impotent threats and ridiculous falacies, and let them know that the Little selfish cry of an Individual is not to be heard when the loud sounds of the people's are publishing their wrongs.

Signed by order.

Charles Cummings, Ch'm.

Calendar of Virginia State Papers 4:34–36

B Response of the Franklinites to the Repeal of the North Carolina Cession Act [1785]

The State of Franklin

William Cage and Others to Gov. Alex Martin
Jonesborough, 22nd March, 1785.

Sir:

Your letter of the 27th of February, 1785, to his Excellency Governor Sevier, favored by Major Henderson, was laid before the Genl, Assembly of the State of Franklin by the Governor.

We think it our duty to communicate to you the sense of the people of this State. We observe your Excellency's candour in informing us that the reason North Carolina repealed the Cession Act was because the Sense of Congress was to allow the State of North Carolina Nothing for the land Ceded. The truth of that assertion we will not undertake to determine; But we humbly Conceive the terms on which Congress was Impowered to accept the Cession was fuly expressed in the Cession Act itself, consequently every reason existed for not passing the Cession act that could have existed for the repeal, Except that of doing Justice to the United States in General, who, upon every principal of Natural Justice, are equally intitled to the land that had been Conquered by our own Joint Efforts.

132

We humbly thank North Carolina for every sentiment of regard she has for us; but are sorry to observe that it is founded upon principles of Interest, as is apparent from the tenor of your Excellency's letter; we are therefore doubtful when the cause ceases which is the basis of your affection we shall consequently loose your esteem.

Sir, Reflect upon the language of some of the most eminent members of the Genl. Assembly of North Carolina at the last Spring session, when the Members from the Western Country were supplicating to be continued a part of your State; were not these their epithets: The inhabitants of the Western Country are the off scourings of the Earth, fugitives from Justice, & we will be rid of them at any rate. The Members of the Western Country, upon hearing these unjust reproaches & being convinced it was the Sense of the Genl. Assembly to get rid of them, Consulted each other & Concluded it was best to appear reconciled with the Masses in order to obtain the best terms they could, & was much astonished to see North Carolina immediately on passing the Act of Cession, center into resolve to Stop the Goods that they, by Act of the Genl. Assembly, had promised to give the Indians for the lands they had taken from them & sold for the Use of the State. The inadequate allowance made the Judges who were appointed to attend the Courts of Criminal Justice, and who had to travel over the Mountains, amounted to prohibition as to the administration of Justice in this quarter, and altho' the Judge appointed on this Side of the Mountains might, from the regard he had to the administration of Justice in the Cumberland Country, have held a Court there; yet, as your Excellency failed to grant him a Commission Agreeable to the Act of Assembly, he could not have performed that Service had he been ever so desirous of doing it. In Short, the Western Country found themselves taxed to support Government, while they were deprived of all the blessings of it. Not to Mention the injustice done them in taxing their lands which lie five hundred miles from trade equal to land of the same quallity on the sea shore. The frequent murders committed by the Indians on our frontiers have Compelled us to think on some plan for our defence. How far North Carolina have been accessary to these Murdours we will not pretend to say. We only know she took the lands the Indians claimed, promised to pay them for it & again resolved Not to do it, & that in consequence of that resolve, the goods Were Stoped.

You say it has been suggested that the Indian goods are to be Seized & the Commisioners arrested when they arrive on the business of the treaty. We are happy to inform you that that Suggestion is false, Groundless & Without the least foundation, & we are Certain you cannot pretend to fault us that the Goods are Stoped by resolve of the Assembly of your State, and if your State are determined to evade their promise to the Indians, we intreat you not to lay the blame upon us, who are intirely innocent & determined to remain so. It is true, we have declared ourselves a free & Independent State & pledged our honours, confirmed by a Solemn Oath, to Support, Maintain & defend the same; But we had not the Most distant Idea that we should have incurred the least displeasure from North Carolina, who compelled us to the measure, & to convince her that we still retain our affection for her, the first law we enacted was to secure & confirm all the rights granted under the laws of North Carolina in the same manner as if we had not declared ourselves an Independent State, have patronized her Constitution & laws & hope her assistance & influence in Congress to precipate our reception into the Federal Union. Should our sanguine hoped be blasted, we are determined never to desert that Independence which we are bound by every Sacred tie of honour & religion to support. We are induced to think North Carolina will not blame us for indeavouring to promote our own Interest & happiness, while we do not attempt to abridge hers, & appeal to the impartial World to determine whether we have deserted North Carolina or North Carolina deserted us.

You will please to lay these our Sentiments before the General Assembly, whome we beg leave to assure that should they ever need our assistance, we shall always be ready to render them every service in our powers, & hope to find the same Sentiments prevailing in them towards us, & we hereunto anex the reason that induced the Convention to a declaration of Independence, which are as follows:

1st. That the constitution of North Carolina declare that it shall be Justifiable to erect New States Westward when ever the consent of the Legislature shall Countinance it, and this Consent is implied we conceive in the Cession Act, which has thrown us into such a situation that the Influence of the law in Common Cases became almost a Nullity & in criminal Jurisdiction had intirely ceased, which reduced us to the verge of Anarchy.

2nd. The Assembly of North Carolina have detained a Certain quantity of Goods which was promised to satisfy the Indians for the lands we possess, which datanure we fully conceive has so exasperated them that they have actually Committed hostilities upon us, & we are alone impeled to defend our selves from their raviges.

3rd. The resolutions of Congress held out from time to time

incouraging the erection of New States have appeared to us ample incouragement.

4th. Our local Situation is such that we not ony apprehend we should be separated from North Carolina, But almost every sensible disinterested traveler had declared it incompatible with our Interest to belong in Union with the Eastern part of the State, For we are not only far removed from the Eastern parts of North Carolina, But Separated from them by high & almost impasable Mountains, which Naturally divide us from them; have proved to us that our Interest is also in many respects distinct from the inhabitants on the other Side & much injured by a Union with them.

5thly. We unanimously agree that our lives, liberties & Property Can be more secure & our happiness Much better propagated by our separation, & Consequently that it is our duty & unalianable right to form ourselves into a New Independent State.

We beg leave to Subscribe ourselves,

Your Excellency's Most Obedient Humbl Servt's,

William Cage, S.C.

Landon Carter, S.S.

By order of the General Assembly.

Thomas Talbot, C.S.

Thomas Chapman, C.C.

Endorsement:

Legislature of the State of Franklin.

Dated, 22nd March, 1785.

Registered & Examined.

No. 1. Tomorrow, 8th D.

State Records of North Carolina, 22:637–640

C A Manifesto,
State of North Carolina [1785]

By his Excellency Alexander Martin, Esquire, Governor, Captain, General and Commander in Chief of the said State

To the Inhabitants of the Counties of Washington, Sullivan and Greene

Whereas, I have received Letters from Brigadier General Sevier, under the style and character of Governor, and from Messrs. Landon Carter and William Cage as speakers of the Senate and Commons of the State of Franklin, informing me that they, with you, the Inhabitants of part of the territory late ceded to congress, had declared themselves independent of the State of North Carolina, and no longer considered themselves under the Sovereignty and jurisdiction of the same; stating their reasons for their separation and revolt, among which it is alleged that the western Country was ceded to Congress without their consent by an Act of the Legislature, and the same was repealed in the like manner....

...The last Assembly having learned what uneasiness and discontent the Cession act had occasioned throughout the State, whose inhabitants had not been previously consulted on that measure, in whom by the Constitution the soil and territorial rights of the State are particularly vested, judging the said Act impolitick at this time, more especially as it would, for a small consideration, dismember the State of one-half of her territory, and in the end tear from her a respectable

Body of her Citizens, when no one State in the Union had parted with any of her Citizens or given any thing like an equivalent to congress but vacant lands of an equivocal and disputed title and distant Situation; and also considering that the said Act by its Tenor and purport was revocable at any time before the Cession should be completed by the Delegates, repealed it by a great majority. At the same time, the Assembly, to convince the people of the Western Country of their affection and attention to their interest, attempted to render Government as easy as possible to them by removing the only general inconvenience and grievance they might labour under, for want of a regular administration of criminal Justice and as proper and immediate command of the Militia, a new District was erected, an assistant judge and a Brigadier General were appointed....

The particular attention the Legislature have paid to the Interest of the Western citizens, though calculated to conciliate their affection and esteem, has not been satisfactory it seems; but the same has been attributed to interest and lucrative designs....

In Order therefore to reclaim such Citizens, who by specious pretences, and the Acts of designing Men, have been seduced from their allegience; to restrain others from following their example who are wavering, and to confirm the attachment and affection of those who adhere to the old Government, and whose fidelity hath not yet been shaken, I have thought proper to issue this manifesto hereby warning all persons concerned in the said revolt that they return to their duty and allegiance, and forbear paying any obedience to any self-created power and authority unknown to the Constitution of the State, and not sanctified by the Legislature. That they and you consider the consequences that may attend such a dangerous and unwarrantable procedure; that far less causes have deluged States and Kingdoms with blood, which at length have been particularly wounded by seizing that by violence, which in time would no doubt have been obtained by consent, when the terms of separation could have been explained and stipulated to the mutual satisfaction of the Mother and new State. That congress, by the Confederation, cannot countenance such a separation wherein the State of North Carolina hath not given her full consent; and if an implied or conditional one hath been given, the same hath been rescinded by a full Legislature, of the reason of so doing they considered themselves the only competent Judges.

That you tarnish not the laurels you have so Gloriously won at King's Mountain, and elsewhere in supporting the freedom and Independence of the United States, and of this in particular, to be whose

Citizens were then your boast, in being concerned in a black and traitrous revolt from that Government in whose defence you have so copiously bled, and which by solemn Oath you are still bound to support. . . .

That you be not insulted or lead away with the pageantry of a mock Government, without the essentials, the shadow without the substance, which always dazzles weak minds, and which will in its present form and manner of existence not only subject you to the ridicule and contempt of the World in general, but rouze the indignation of the other States in the Union at your obtruding yourselves as a power among them without their consent. . . . Let your representatives come forward and present every grievance in a Constitutional manner that they may be redressed, and let your terms of separation be proposed with decency; your proportion of the public debts ascertained, the vacant territory appropriated, to the mutual benefit of both parties in such manner and proportion, as may be just and reasonable. Let your proposals be consistant with the honor of the State to acceed to, which by your allegiance as good Citizens you cannot violate, and I make no doubt her generosity in time will meet your wishes.

But, on the contrary, should you be hurried on by blind ambition to pursue your present unjustifiable measures, which may open afresh the wounds of this late bleeding Country, and plunge it again into all the miseries of a Civil Warr, which God avert, let the fatal consequences be charged on the authors. It is only time which can reveal the event. I know with reluctance the State will be driven to arms; it will be the last alternative to embrue her hands in the blood of her Citizens; but if no other ways and means are found to save her honor, and reclaim her headstrong refractory Citizens but this last sad expedient, her resources are not Yet so exhausted, or her spirits damped but she may take satisfaction for this great injury received, regain her Government over the revolted territory, or render it not worth possessing. But all these effects may be prevented at this time by removing the causes; by those who have revolted to return to their duty, and those who have stood firm still to continue to support the Government of this State until the consent of the Legislature be fully and constitutionally had for a separate Sovereignty and jurisdiction. All which, by virtue of the powers and authorities which your representatives and others of the State at large have invested me with in General Assembly, I hereby Will, Command and require, as you will be liable to answer all the pains and Penalties that may ensue on the Contrary.

Given under Hand and the Great seal of the State, which I have caused to be hereunto affixed at Hillsborough, the twenty-fifth Day of April, in the year of our Lord, one thousand seven hundred and eighty-five, and ninth year of the Independence of the said State.

Alex Martin

By His Excellency's Command.
James Glasgow, Sec.
Endorsement: Manifesto
State Records of North Carolina, 22:642–647

D An Association Drawn Up by the Secessionists of Washington County, Virginia [1785]

Presented to the Confederation Congress in January, 1785

We the inhabitants of the Country Westward of the Allegany Mountains taking into serious consideration the present exigency of our affairs, have agreed to, and will support the following resolutions.

1st RESOLVED that any number of people under any government have an indefensible right to consult and provide for their proper interests, to assert and maintain their proper rights and to represent and remedy their real grievances.

2nd RESOLVED that as every citizen has a right to emigrate from one state or Government to another, in pursuit of happiness; so any number of citizens in any state may justly endeavour to introduce such alteration in their present situation and government as they think will increase their happiness or remove their uneasiness where they live.

3rd RESOLVED that as individuals are not created for the pleasure of government, but government is instituted for the happiness of the individuals, therefore the lands which be cultivated by individuals belong strictly to them and not to the government, otherwise every citizen would be a tenant and not a landlord, a vassal and not a freeman; and every government would be a usurpation not an instrument and device for the publick good. For cogent is the reasoning when we can with great truth say our own blood was spilt in acquiring lands for our settlement, our fortunes expended in making those settlements effectual for ourselves we fought, for ourselves we conquered, and for ourselves alone we have a right to hold.

4th RESOLVED that it is the duty of every American citizen to entertain a sacred regard for the principles of the continental union, because this union is the only security of the independency of each of the united states, as well as of that spirit of freedom upon which the government of each state is to be maintained respectively. That therefore we will ever display an ardent zeal for those generous principles of union and be ready to resign all partial considerations of private interest or the interest of particular states when they would undermine the interests of the confederacy, and endanger the glorious privileges which the confederacy is designed to defend and preserve.

Papers of the Continental Congress,
Micro Copy no. 247, Roll 62, Item 48, p. 287.

E A Second Petition Drawn Up by the Separatists of Washington County, Virginia, April 7, 1785

Presented to the Confederation Congress

Sir,

The Deputies of the good People of this County being deeply impressed with a sense of the situation of their Constituents; the value of their Civil and Religious Rights; with the advantages of local Constitutions; and the American Union: They cannot remain indifferent Spectators of measures that must eventually affect their dearest interests.

We have maturely considered several Acts of Congress respecting the Western Country; and have been constant observers of the Proceedings of some of the Southern States, claiming jurisdiction over it; and the result of our inquiries and observations are; that the Western Inhabitants, can no longer be safe or useful in Society, without the protecting Arm of the federal government, and the privileges of an independent State.

The thinking part of the Community are particularly anxious to part with the ancient Stock the eastern parts of Virginia in friendship and good humor, to introduce and maintain a receprocity of kind offices with her and in reality be one People in a national view.

When we turn our eyes to the Acts of your honorable Body, our prospects are enlarged; The Articles in that of the Twenty third day of April last, will form a basis for a liberal and beneficial Compact; we are sorry to object to it, in the smallest tittle, were it not that we know, we were not represented when those Resolves were formed; and we trust, that congress on an attentive revision of the subject, will conclude, that natural boundaries will be most convenient and satisfactory, especially when they nearly coincide with the Meridians and Parallels already held out, as boundaries for the new States.

That meridian that crosses the Ohio at the west Cape of the Kanhawa is a striking instance; for to the South, it will pass over a great number of the most inaccessable and craggy Mountains in America; and we have reason to believe it will intersect the Kanhawa in various places, notwithstanding its being otherwise expressed in some Maps; Whereas had that river been adopted as a boundary; expence, trouble and inconveniency might have been avoided, and both sides reap equal advantages. We will avoid using argument, why the Siota and Sandusky may not be substituted in place of a Meridian, on the North side of the Ohio.

We beg leave further to represent, – that the Parallel of thirty seven degrees, and the Meridian that passes the Ohio at the Rapids, would be inconvenient in several respects.

The Valleys adjoining the Kanhawa, above or south of the Ronceverte or Green-briar river, lies most convenient to those under latitude thirty six, on the heads of the Cherokee river. That the parallel of thirty seven extended to the Meridian of the Rapids, would sever the Kentucky Settlements, and be too far removed from whose on the Holstein.

Indulge us Sir, to mention what we believe would be the most convenient, and equitable limits of two new States. Let that which will include the Kentuckey Settlements be bounded on the East, by the great Kanhawa, as high as the confluence of the Ronceverte; the Ohio on the North; and on the West and South, by a Meridian line drawn from the Mouth of Salt River, until it intersects the Shawanoe or Cumberland river, up that river to the mouth of that branch of it, called Rock-Castle, up the said River Rock-Castle to the Ausioto or Brush-Mountain, thence a direct line to the confluence of the Ronceverte.

That to the South which will include the Inhabitants on the heads of Kanhawa and Cherokee rivers, be bounded by a line extended due South from that part of the Cumberland river where the Meidian lie drawn from the mouth of Salt-river will touch it until it reaches Elk-river, down that river to the Tenasee, thence South to the top of the

Apalachian Mountain, eastwardly along the same to a point, from whence a north line extended, would meet the Kanhawa at the mouth of Little-river, near Ingles-Ferry; and down that River to the Ronceverte westwardly along the boundary as above described for the Kentuckey Country.

At this day, we find a new Society forming itself back of North-Carolina, which, if the requisition of Congress of the twenty ninth day of April last, is regarded, we of course will be annexed to, and the natural situation of the Country points out the connection; but are yet restrained, from formally joining them, by a deference to the opinions of those that bear rule in Virginia; and the want of an orderly accession to Independence under the auspices of Congress; these obstacles we confide, that the Rulers of the federal Government will remove. The interest of America seems urgently to call for it, and the peace and prosperity of the Western Inhabitants, will no longer admit of delay....

We have the honor to be, with all due deference and Respect,

> Your Excellency's most obedient
> and devoted humble Servants.

Signed by Order,
Chas. Cummings, Ch.

> *Papers of the Contenintal Congress*
> Micro Copy no. 247, Roll 62, Item 48, pp. 297–390

F Letter to a Young Man

Written by Arthur Campbell to His Nephew, David Campbell [1799]

Sir,

At a time when the attention of not only Individuals but also that of whole States are drawn towards the fundamental principles of government, from an alarm that our liberties are in danger, it may not be unacceptable to offer some observations, and opinions that may be useful in forming a right judgement of public men and public measures on which so much depends at this time.

Democrat and Aristocrat are appellations not unfrequently given, by one party to the other, and both claiming the name of Republican, without either affixing a determinate idea of the terms or defining the characteristics of republicanism.

Democracy among the ancient nations hath been defined to be a government where the supreme power is lodged with the people, and exercised by them. This form of government has been deemed most consonant to the order of nature, and the freedom of Man; it has been successfully administered in small communities, but in large and opulent associations, men soon degenerate to anarchy, for under the pleasing name of liberty, licentiousness is introduced, which is only another name for despotism. Licentiousness is the dominion of passion and caprice and violence. It is a contempt of law, right, and justice, as much as arbitrary rule can possible be.

Aristocracy has been called a government by the nobles or where the supreme power was lodged with a few and for life and often hereditary. This form would place on one side all honor and respect, and nothing but disregard and contempt on the other, here all appreciation and violence, and there all patience and submission, here all convenience and pleasure, and there all labour and indigence.

As to Monarchy or kingly power, it is altogether inadmissible. In democracies, the people may govern well, while a sense of present danger[s] are hanging over them, or where they reverence virtue as the chief good, and abhor vice as the worse of evils; Aristocracy may be long upheld, when a sense of honor pervades the body politic, where talents, integrity and the love of order, are deemed more necessary than wealth. But an indivdual invested with the whole sovereign power, can not from the narrowness of the human mind, extend his views to every department of civil society. He will unavoidably be exposed to imposition from some quarter or other, even when it is pre-supposed that he is endowed with strong traits of wisdom and goodness. His administration of consequence can never be marked with that extensive beneficence which results from a *representative government*. It is latter from which is best calculated to collect into one point the wisdom, ingenuity and vigour, which are diffused through the whole social body. But in monarchies when the prince is a tyrant, the names of master and slave annihiliate all claims of duty, all voluntary offerings of affection and patriotism, and exhibit man to man in a state of warfare, whence power is the only right and terror the only obligation. Men may from a sense of fear submit in silence to a king, yet they abhor him in their hearts. Every such ruler must share all the terror he inspires and *join trembling with his commands*. Knowing himself the enemy of mankind, he can place no confidence in their affections, and make no appeal to their justice.

The *Republican Plan*, or modern republics, particularly that in America, unites the essentials of each of the above forms, and calls it a representative or mixed government: or what it might without arrogance assume the name of a *real republic*. For under the Constitution of the United States, every honest station of life is honorable, since they are all parts of the great social body. Between the Chief Magistrate, and the people, the great and the mean the rich and the poor, the acute and the dull, the learned and the ignorant, there is no difference, as to the rights of citizenship, but in possession of different powers, and in the discharge of different offices, peculiar to each capacity and useful to all. And if one of them have a just demand for submission and obedience, for honor and respect, for convenience and ease, the other have as just a claim for protection and defence, for the administration of justice and the preservation of equal liberty, for the supply of their wants and the relief of their distresses, for *instruction* and *good example*.

From what is already said, you may have a better understanding of the terms *Aristocrat* and *Democrat*, so much used in France in the first years of her Revolution and lately applied to designate parties in America. You will see on the one hand, that all men are not equal in rights, but only when they mutually perform their *duties*, and that the declaration—"That all men are by nature equally free and independent. That when they enter into a state of society they divest themselves of a portion of their liberty to secure the rest,"—is not correct. For how can we conclude that all men by nature are equal, when daily experience evince that one is stronger another weaker, one wise, some foolish, one beautiful another deformed, one dull another ingenious. And we are equally at a loss to understand the arguments in support of the position: That when men enter into a state of society they divest themselves of a portion of what nature has bestowed. Does entering into a state of Society require that a man put off a part of his wit, strength, beauty or ingenuity? The fact is, that we divest ourselves of nothing, but the power to *commit wrongs*, and enter into a state to *improve every thing*, that form a natural *inequality* may spring a perfect *equality* in respect of every moral and social obligation. Thus instead of losing be entering into a state of society, we are great gainers; every mental power can better be drawn forth, and acquire an energy in useful exertions. The very corporeal faculties increase in vigour and desterity.

It is therefore true that in forming the social body, there must be superiors, inferiors and equals, but as in the natural body, the hands can not say to the feet we have no need of thee, so in the social, the *head* and *heart* can not say to the rest of the members, we can do as well without you.

Thus the grand principle of equality of obligation and of mutual dependence, if adopted in opinion, as it is established in nature, would show the true ground of distinctions among men. If stations and officers are netiher unjustly *usurped*, nor their duties perfidiously and *weakly* performed, the obligation to obedience and submission, is as strong on inferiors, as that of justice and disinterested zeal, for the public good is on rulers and magistrates, and the honor obtained by distinguished abilities is equally due to their possessors, as the fruits of their honest labour are due to the lower order of the community.

Our Representative plan places the fabric of society on a firm and lasting foundation, and all the parts of the building however different in point of use or ornament, are so closely connected, and so necessary to the whole, that none of them can be removed, or defaced, without injuring the beauty or the solidity of the structure. A constant balance and reaction of obligation and duty are thus maintained through all the departments of society, similar to what we are in nature. These are the principles on which modern republics ought to be founded. This is that liberty and equality, to which all may aspire, without any danger of disorganizing the *body politic*. It is the system which men may not only talk about, but live up to. It may well be called a representative government, it is real republicanism.

But unfortunately for the happiness of the human race, these are principles, which turbulent and designing men may seek to abuse, as an engine for overturning order and good government, and for introducing that *anarchy* in the midst of which they may be gainers.

In a representative government, there is an *equality*, but it implies subordination, an *equality* of wants with a diversity of means of supplying them, an *equality* of obligation with different modes of discharging it. It is an *equality* which by rendering all equally necessary, makes all who faithfuly discharge their duties equally acceptable in the sight of God, but by requiring higher and lower stations and various distinctions and spheres, establishes different degrees of respectability and honor among men. It is an *equality* that degrades none but the tyrant, the ruffian, the thief, the voluptuary, and the shaggard and exalts all but these, to the ennobling dignity of constituent members of the grand community of mankind and fellow labourers with God in advancing the felicity of his moral and intellectual creation. Liberty, equality, legitimate rule, and protection, are all thus harmoniously combined to affect the end of national association. The *public good*—where *rights* are claimed, *duties* must be performed, where submission and obedience are demanded, an obligation is implied for the *Trustee*, to be wise and faithful. In fine all governments, all associations, whether religious or civil, can only rightfully subsist when there are a receprocity of obligation of duty, but more especially, a representative civil association, where inalienable and important rights are to be preserved on one hand, and necessary duties to be observed on the other. When all this is done, liberty, equality, safety, and happiness, will be the certain result. *It is an imitation of the Diety, in his government of the World.* As the above can not be deemed a theoretical plan, but is altogether practical and salutary in common life, equally removed from furious jacobinism and chilling aristocracy, it holds out motives for exertions to those whose talents and opportunities may designate them for conspicuous stations in society and rewards for all who aspire to the title of being useful citizens of the American commonwealth.

Accept, Sir, this offering of my affectionate regard.

Arthur Campbell

Arthur Campbell to David Campbell, January 29, 1799, David Campbell Papers.

Chapter Notes

1. Bearing the Yoke

1. David Campbell to Lyman C. Draper, Dec. 12, 1840, Lyman C. Draper Collection, 10DD6, State Historical Society of Wisconsin. Microfilm copy, University of Georgia Library, Athens, Georgia.

2. David Campbell to Draper, Feb. 16, 1843, Draper Mss., 10DD36.

3. David Campbell to Draper, Feb. 1, 1843, Draper Mss., 10DD34. In this letter, Campbell quotes what William Martin said about Arthur Campbell.

4. Draper to William Martin, Feb. 18, 1843, Draper Mss., 3XX14.

5. William B. Campbell to Draper, Jan. 9, 1842, Draper Mss., 10DD15.

6. Lewis Preston Summers, *History of Southwest Virginia, 1746–1786, Washington County, 1777–1870* (Richmond, Va.: J.L. Hill Printing Company, 1903), p. 67. (Hereinafter referred to as Summers, *Southwest Virginia.*)

7. Samuel Cole Williams, *History of the Lost State of Franklin* (Johnson City, Tenn.: Watauga Press, 1924), p. 287. (Hereinafter referred to as Williams, *State of Franklin.*)

8. *Ibid.*, p. 286.

9. Leslie Lyle Campbell, *The Campbell Clan in Virginia* (Lexington, Va.: n.p., 1954), p. 21. (Hereinafter referred to as Campbell, *Campbell Clan.*)

10. Hugh Blair Grigsby, *The Virginia Convention of 1776* (Richmond, Va.: J.W. Randolph, 1855), p. 202. Microfilm, University of Georgia, Athens. (Hereinafter referred to as Grigsby, *Convention of 1776.*)

11. David Campbell to Draper, Dec. 12, 1840, Draper Mss., 10DD6.

12. *Ibid.*

13. *Ibid.*; Marcus Lee Hansen, *The Atlantic Migration 1607–1860: A History of the Continuing Settlement of the United States* (New York: Harper and Row, Publishers, 1961), p. 27. (Hereinafter referred to as Hansen, *Atlantic Migration.*)

14. Hansen, *Atlantic Migration*, p. 27.

15. Henry Jones Ford, *The Scotch-Irish in America* (Princeton, N.J.: Princeton University Press, 1951), pp. 181–184.

16. *Ibid.*, p. 185–187; David Hawke, *The Colonial Experience* (New York: Bobbs Merrill Company, Inc., 1966), p. 368. (Hereinafter referred to as Hawke, *Colonial Experience.*)

17. Hawke, *Colonial Experience*, p. 367; Carl Lotus Becker, *Beginnings of the American People* (Boston: Houghton Mifflin, 1915; reprint ed., Ithaca, N.Y.: Cornell University, 1966), p. 19.

18. Campbell, *Campbell Clan*, p. 16.

19. Margaret Campbell Pilcher, *Historical Sketches of the Campbell, Pilcher and Kindred Families, Including the Bowen, Faliaferre, and Powell Families* (Nashville, Tenn.: Press of Marshall & Bruce Co., 1911), p. 23. (Hereinafter referred to as Pilcher, *Historical Sketches.*)

20. Campbell, *Campbell Clan*, p. 17; Pilcher, *Historical Sketches*, p. 12.

21. Joseph A. Waddell, *Annals of Augusta County, Virginia* (Richmond, Va.: Wm. Ellis Jones, Book and Job Printer, 1886), p. 13. (Hereinafter referred to as Waddell, *Augusta County.*)

22. William W. Hening, ed., *The Status at Large; Being a Collection of all the Laws of Virginia from the First Session of the Legislature, in the Year 1619*, 13 vols. (Richmond, Va.: Franklin Press, 1820), 5: 78–79. (Hereinafter referred to as Hening, *Statutes.*) Lyman Chalkley, ed., *Chronicles of the Scotch-Irish Settlement in Virginia*, 3 vols. (Baltimore, Md.: Genealogical Publishing Co., 1965), 1:13.

23. David Campbell to Draper, Dec. 12, 1840, Draper Mss., 10DD6.

24. Pilcher, *Historical Sketches*, p. 22.

25. David Campbell to Draper, Dec. 12, 1840, Draper Mss., 10DD6.

26. There is some disagreement as to Arthur Campbell's birth date. This is the date inscribed on Campbell's tombstone, by the authority of his son Arthur Lee. See Robert L. Kincaid, "Colonel Arthur Campbell:

Frontier Leader and Patriot," *The Historical Society of Washington County, Virginia, Publications*, Series II, no. 1 (Fall, 1965): 18. (Hereinafter referred to as Kincaid, "Arthur Campbell.") Summers, *Southwest Virginia*, p. 463; David Campbell to Draper, Dec. 29, 1842. Draper Mss., 10DD25.

27. Pilcher, *Historical Sketches*, pp. 33–34; Campbell, *Campbell Clan*, pp. 19–20.

28. David Campbell to Draper, Dec. 12, 1840, Draper Mss., 10DD6.

29. David Campbell to Draper, Jan. 16, 1843, Draper Mss., 10DD30.

30. Charles E. Kemper, "The Settlement of the Valley," *Virginia Magazine of History and Biography*, 30 (January, 1922): 179.

31. James Smith, *An Account of the Remarkable Occurrences in the Life and Travels of Col. James Smith* (Lexington: John Bradford, 1799), p. 29. Microcard copy, University of Georgia. (Hereinafter referred to as Smith, *Remarkable Occurrences*.) Smith states that while he and Arthur Campbell were prisoners of the Wyandottes, Arthur read the Bible. At this time he was about 15 years old.

32. Williams, *State of Franklin*, p. 285.

33. Thomas C. Wilson, Jr., ed., *Washington and Lee University Alumni Directory, 1749–1940* (Lexington, Va.: Washington and Lee University Alumni, Inc., 1949), p. 42.

34. Kincaid, "Arthur Campbell," p. 9.

35. Quoted in Oscar T. Barck, Jr., and Hugh T. Lefler, *Colonial America* (London: Collier-Macmillan Limited, 1969), pp. 441–448. (Hereinafter referred to as Bark and Lefler, *Colonial America*.) John C. Fitzpatrick, ed., *The Diaries of George Washington, 1748–1799*, 4 vols. (Boston: Houghton Mifflin Company, 1925), 1: 43–101.

36. Bark and Lefler, *Colonial America*, pp. 450–451.

37. Henry Howe, *Historical Collections of Virginia* (Charleston, S.C.: Babcock & Company, 1845), p. 96. (Hereinafter referred to as Howe, *Virginia*.)

38. Francis Parkman, *The Conspiracy of Pontiac and the Indian War After the Conquest of Canada*, 2 vols. (Boston: Little, Brown, and Company, 1902), 1: 115–120. (Hereinafter referred to as Parkman, *Conspiracy of Pontiac*.)

39. *Ibid.*; Alexander Scott Withers, *Chronicles of Border Warfare or A History of the Settlement by the Whites of Northwestern Virginia and the Indian*

Wars and Massacres (Clarksburg, Va.: Published by Joseph Israel, 1831), p. 53. Microcard copy, University of Georgia Library. (Hereinafter referred to as Withers, *Border Warfare*.) Howe, *Virginia*, p. 98.

40. Parkman, *Conspiracy of Pontiac*, 1, 114.

41. Hening, *Statutes*, 6, 465.

42. John Lewis Peyton, *History of Augusta County, Virginia*, 2nd ed. (Bridgewater, Va., n.p., 1953), p. 6.

43. Withers, *Border Warfare*, p. 77–79.

44. John Pendleton Kennedy, ed., *Journals of the House of Burgesses of Virginia, 1761–1765*, 13 vols. (Richmond, Va.: The Colonial Press, 1907), p. 324.

45. Withers, *Border Warfare*, pp. 72–73; See map in Wadell, *Augusta County*, p. 82; Louis K. Koontz, "The Virginia Frontier, 1754–1863," *Johns Hopkins University Studies in Historical and Political Science*, 40 (no. 2 1925): 148.

46. Withers, *Border Warfare*, pp. 72–73.

47. Smith, *Remarkable Occurrences*, p. 29.

48. The account of Campbell's captivity has been taken from a number of sources, the most useful of which are the correspondence between David Campbell and Lyman C. Draper and a sketch of Arthur Campbell by John Campbell, Treasurer of the United States during Andrew Jackson's administration in the 1830's. They can be found in the Draper Mss., 10DD42, 10DD43, 10DD54, 10DD66, 10DD68, 10DD73, and in Howe, *Virginia*, pp. 503–504. All of these sources state that Campbell was captured at Dickenson's Fort on Cowpasture River. Recent writers have taken the same position. However, a petition of Arthur Campbell's was presented to the House of Burgesses, on May 5, 1765, "setting forth that on the 14th of September, 1758, he joined a company of ranges, under the command of Capt. John Dickenson, stationed at Fort Young in Augusta County, where he was unfortunately captivated, and detained a prisoner until December the 25th, 1760, and by that means not returned in Capt. Dickenson's Pay Roll; and praying the consideration of the House." The Committee of Claims considered the petition and on May 8, the House resolved "that Arthur Campbell ought to be allowed by the Publick the Sum of £41 for his Pay as a Ranger, during his captivity by the Enemy." See Kennedy, *Burgesses, 1761–1765*, pp. 324, 328.

49. Howe, *Virginia*, p. 504.

50. Governor Dunmore to the Surveyor of Fincastle, Dec. 15, 1773, Arthur Campbell Papers, Microfilm, Filson Club, Louisville, Kentucky.

2. On the Holston

1. Bark and Lefler, *Colonial America*, pp. 475–482; Warren M. Billings, John E. Selby, and Thad W. Tate, *Colonial Virginia: A History* (White Plains, N.Y.: KTO Press, 1986), p. 287.

2. Theodore Roosevelt, *The Winning of the West*, 4 vols. (New York: G.P. Putnam's Sons, 1897), 1: 168–169. (Hereinafter referred to as Roosevelt, *West*.)

3. David Campbell to Lyman C. Draper, Jan. 12, 1843, Draper Mss., 3QQ30; Goodridge Wilson, *Smyth County History and Traditions* (Radford, Va.: Commonwealth Press, Inc., 1932), pp. 16–19. (Hereinafter referred to as Wilson, *Smyth County*.) Elizabeth Lemmon Sayers, *Pathfinders and Patriots* (Marion, Va.: Smyth County Historical and Museum Society, Inc., 1983) pp. 103–108. (Hereinafter referred to as Sayers, *Pathfinders*.) Sayers notes Arthur moved from his original log home to a nearby "double log house," called "Goodwood."

4. Jack M. Sosin, *The Revolutionary Frontier, 1763–1783* (New York: Holt, Rinehart and Winston, 1967), p. 74. (Hereinafter referred to as Sosin, *Revolutionary Frontier*.) Sayers, *Pathfinders*, pp. 114, 117, 145. Howard McKnight Wilson, *Great Valley Patriots: Western Virginia in the Struggle for Liberty* (Verona, Va.: McClure Printing Company, Inc., 1976), pp. 3–12. (Hereinafter referred to as Wilson, *Patriots*.) See the "Key to Places of Interest" on the inside cover of Wilson's *Patriots*.

5. Hening, *Statutes*, VIII, 395–396.

6. *Ibid.*, p. 600.

7. Campbell to Draper, Dec. 12, 1840, Draper Mss., 10DD6. Margaret Campbell was the sister of William Campbell.

8. *Ibid.*

9. *Fincastle County Virginia Court Records, Order Book 1, 1773–1788*, January 5, 1773. Microfilm copy, Virginia State Library, Richmond.

10. Summers, *Southwest Virginia*, p. 138.

11. There were 15 justices commissioned for Fincastle County December 1, 1772, Summers, *Southwest Virginia*, p. 130.

12. Oliver Perry Chitwood, "Justice in Colonial Virginia," *Johns Hopkins University Studies in Historical and Political Science*, 23 (July–August, 1905): 472-474. (Hereinafter referred to as Chitwood, "Justice.")

13. *Botetourt County Virginia Court Order Book I, 1770-1771*, March 12, 1770. Microfilm copy, Virginia State Library, Richmond; Summers, *Southwest Virginia*, p. 109.

14. Summers, *Southwest Virginia*, p. 137.

15. Chitwood, "Justice," p. 492.

16. *Fincastle Court Records Order Book I*, p. 7.

17. Louis Phelps Kellogg, "Cornstalk," *Dictionary of American Biography*, 17 vols., eds., Allen Johnson, et al. (New York: Charles Scribner's Sons, 1964-1981) 2: 447-448. (Hereinafter referred to as Kellogg, "Cornstalk.")

18. *Fincastle County Virginia Recordbook of Deeds*, p. 227. Microfilm copy, Virginia State Library, Richmond.

19. Thomas Perkins Abernethy, *Western Lands and the American Revolution* (New York: D. Appleton-Century Company, 1937), p. 103. (Hereinafter referred to as Abernethy, *Western Lands*.)

20. Rueben Gold Thwaites and Louise Phelps Kellogg, *Documentary History of Dunmore's War, 1774* (Madison: Wisconsin Historical Society, 1905), p. 14. (Hereinafter referred to as Thwaites and Kellogg *Dunmore's War*.) Constance Lindsay Skinner, *Pioneers of the Old Southwest* (New York: United States Publishing Association, Inc., 1919), pp. 117-118. (Hereinafter referred to as Skinner, *Pioneers*.)

21. Lawrence C. Wroth, "James Logan," *Dictionary of American Biography*, 6: 362-363.

22. Quoted in Virgil Anson Lewis, *History of the Battle of Point Pleasant, Fought Between White Men and Indians at the Mouth of the Great Kanawha River (New Point Pleasant, West Virginia) Monday, October 10th, 1774. The Chief Event of Dunmore's War* (Charleston, W. Va.: The Tribune Printing Company, 1909), p. 17.

23. *Ibid.*

24. See the introduction to the Preston Papers, Draper Mss., QQ series.

25. Campbell to Preston, June, 1774. Draper Mss., 3QQ40.

26. Campbell to Preston, June 23, 1774, Draper Mss., 3QQ44.

27. Campbell to Preston, June, 1774, Draper Mss., 3QQ40.

28. Katherine Elizabeth Crane, "Oconostota," *Dictionary of American Biography*. 7: 621-622.

29. Campbell to Preston, June 22, 1774, Draper Mss., 3QQ41.

30. Campbell to Preston, June 23, 1774, Draper Mss., 3QQ44.

31. Frederick Webb Hodge, ed., *Handbook of the American Indians*, Part 1, Bulletin no. 30; *Bureau of American Ethnology* (Washington, D.C.: U.S. Government Printing Office, 1907), p. 115.

32. Campbell to Preston, June 23, 1774, Draper Mss., 3QQ41.

33. Campbell to Preston, August 12, 1774, Draper Mss., 3QQ75.

34. Samuel Cole Williams, "Shelby's Fort," *East Tennessee Historical Society's Publications*, 8 (no. 7, 1935): 30.

35. Campbell to Preston, July 1, 1774, Draper Mss., 3QQ75.

36. Preston to William Christian, July 2, 1774. Draper Mss., 3QQ51.

37. [Campbell to Preston, Early Oct., 1774], Draper Mss. 3QQ111. The first part of the letter is missing, but the content makes it obvious that it was written to Preston.

38. Campbell to Preston, Oct. 6, 1774, Draper Mss., 3QQ106.

39. Campbell to Preston, September 29, 1774, Draper Mss., 3QQ106.

40. Campbell to Preston, Oct. 9, 1774, Draper Mss., 3QQ117. Campbell to Preston, Oct. 12, 1774, Draper Mss., 3QQ118.

41. Kellogg, "Cornstalk," *Dictionary of American Biography*, 3: 447–448.

42. Quoted in Robert L. Kincaid, *The Wilderness Road* (New York: The Bobbs-Merrill Company, 1947), p. 89.

43. *Ibid.*

3. Revolutionary Rumblings

1. Henry Steele Commager and Richard B. Morris, eds., *The Spirit of 'Seventy-Six: The Story of the American Revolution as Told by Participants* (New York: Bonanza Books, 1983), p. 317. (Hereinafter referred to as Commager and Morris, *'Seventy-Six*.) For a convenient primary source tracing the major steps which led to the writing of the Declaration of Independence, see Chapter Eight of *'Seventy-Six*, "The Great Declaration," pp. 271–324.

2. The events leading to the American Revolution can be found in John Richard Alden, *The American Revolution, 1775–1783* (New York: Harper & Row Publishers), pp. 1–15. (Hereinafter referred to as Alden,

Revolution.) John C. Miller, *Origins of the American Revolution* (Stanford, Calif.: Stanford University Press, 1959); Lawrence Henry Gipson, *The Coming of the Revolution, 1763–1775* (New York: Harper & Row Publishers, 1954); Claude H. Van Tyne, *The Causes of the War of Independence* (New York: Peter Smith, 1951); Bark and Lefler, *Colonial America,* pp. 459–469, 490–534.

3. Commager and Morris *'Seventy-Six,* p. 105; H.J. Eckenrode, *The Revolution in Virginia* (Boston: Houghton Mifflin Company, 1916) pp. 125–133. (Hereinafter referred to as Eckenrode, *Revolution in Virginia*); Charles Washington Coleman, "The County Committees of 1774–75 in Virginia," *William and Mary College Quarterly Historical Magazine,* Ser. 1, 5 (October, 1898): 95. (Hereinafter referred to as Coleman, "County Committees.")

4. Coleman, "County Committees," p. 98.

5. Eckenrode, *Revolution in Virginia,* p. 35.

6. Coleman, "County Committees," p. 100.

7. Peter Force, ed., *American Archives: A Documentary History of the English Colonies in North America,* 4th Series, March 7, 1774, to August 21, 1776, 6 vols. (Washington, D.C.: M. St. Clair Clark and Peter Force, 1846), 1, col. 1165. (Hereinafter referred to as Force, *Archives.*)

8. *Ibid.,* col. 1166.

9. Commager and Morris, *'Seventy-Six,* p. 290.

10. Force, *Archives,* Col. 1166.

11. *Ibid.*

12. Eckenrode, *Revolution in Virginia,* p. 38.

13. Sosin, *Revolutionary Frontier,* p. 95.

14. *Ibid.,* p. 94.

15. Richard Barksdale Harwell, ed., *The Committees of Westmoreland and Fincastle: Proceedings of the County Committees, 1774–1776* (Richmond: The Virginia State Library, 1956), p. 86. (Hereinafter referred to as Harwell, *Proceedings.*) Hening, *Statutes,* 10: 195.

16. Commager and Morris, *'Seventy-Six,* pp. 108–109.

17. *Ibid.,* p. 106; John E. Selby, *The Revolution in Virginia, 1775–1783,* (Williamsburg: The Colonial Williamsburg Foundation, 1988), pp. 1–6. (Hereinafter referred to as Selby, *Virginia.*)

18. Bark and Lefler, *Colonial America,* p. 543.

19. Commager and Morris, 'Seventy-Six, p. 106.

20. Summers, Southwest Virginia, p. 207–208.

21. Harwell, Proceedings, p. 64; American Archives, 4th Series, 2, cols. 301–302.

22. American Archives, 4th Series, 2, cols. 1620–1621.

23. Grigsby, Convention of 1776, pp. 202–203.

24. Howe, Virginia, p. 504.

25. American Archives, 4th Series, VI, col. 1513.

26. Arthur Campbell to Timothy Pickering, July 2, 1799, Timothy Pickering Papers, 25, 8, Massachusetts Historical Society Collections, Microfilm copy, University of Georgia Library, Athens, Georgia.

27. American Archives, 4th Series, 6, col. 1534.

28. Grigsby, Convention of 1776, p. 203.

29. American Archives, 4th Series, 6, col. 1534.

30. Brent Tarter and Robert L. Scribner, eds., Revolutionary Virginia: The Road to Independence, Part Two, Independence and the Fifth Convention, 1776: A Documentary Record (Charlottesville: University Press of Virginia, 1983), 7: p. 698. (Hereinafter referred to as Tarter and Scribner, Revolutionary Virginia.) American Archives, 4th Series, 6 col. 1610.

31. Edmund Cody Burnett, The Continental Congress (New York: W.W. Norton & Company, 1964), p. 167.

32. American Archives, 4th Series, 6, col. 1524. Tarter and Scribner, Revolutionary Virginia, Part One, 7: 141–143.

33. Burnett, Continental Congress, p. 170.

34. Worthingtoin Chauncey Ford, ed., Journals of the Continental Congress, 1774–1789, 34 vols. (Washington, D.C.: U.S. Government Printing Office, 1906), 5: 506–507.

35. Quoted in Alden, American Revolution, p. 81.

36. American Archives, 4th Series, 6, cols. 1537.

37. Howe, Virginia, p. 504.

38. Tarter and Scribner, Revolutionary Virginia, Part One, 7: 272; American Archives, 4th Series, 6, col. 1562.

39. Grigsby, *Convention of 1776*, p. 19; *American Archives*, 4th Series, vols. 1592–1598. Tarter and Scribner, *Revolutionary Virginia*, Part Two, 7: 649–656.

40. Robert L. Ganyard, "Threat from the West: North Carolina and the Cherokees, 1776–1778." *The North Carolina Historical Review*, 45 (Winter, 1969): 48.

41. John P. Brown, *Old Frontiers: The Story of the Cherokee Indians from Earliest Times to the Date of Their Removal to the West, 1838* (Kingsport, Tenn.: Southern Publishers, Inc., 1938), p. 139. (Hereinafter referred to as Brown, *Old Frontiers*.)

42. J.G.M. Ramsey, *The Annals of Tennessee to the End of the Eighteenth Century* (Charleston, S.C.: Walker and Jones, 1853; reprint ed., Kingsport, Tenn., Kingsport Press, 1967), p. 163. (Hereinafter referred to as Ramsey, *Annals*.)

43. Harwell, *Proceedings*, pp. 108–109.

44. *American Archives*, 4th Series, 6, col. 1557.

45. Brown, *Old Frontier*, pp. 148–149.

46. *Ibid.*, pp. 151–152.

47. John Haywood, *The Civil and Political History of the State of Tennessee from Its Earliest Settlement up to the Year 1796, Including Boundaries of the State* (Nashville, Tenn.: Publishing House of the Methodist Episcopal Church, South, 1891), p. 65. (Hereinafter referred to as Haywood, *Civil and Political History of Tennessee*.) Samuel Cole Williams, *Tennessee During the Revolutionary War* (Nashville: The Tennessee Historical Commission, 1944), pp. 42–47. (Hereinafter referred to as Williams, *Tennessee*.)

48. William Campbell to Arthur Campbell, August 1, 1776, Draper Mss., 9DD4.

49. Williams, *Tennessee*, p. 50; R.S. Cotterill, *The Southern Indians: The Story of the Civilized Tribes Before Removal* (Norman: University of Oklahoma Press, 1954), pp. 42–45.

50. *Ibid.*, pp. 52–57.

51. Ramsey, *Annals*, pp. 165–174.

4. Father of Washington County

1. Temple Bodley, *George Rogers Clark: His Life and Public Services* (Boston: Houghton Mifflin Company, 1926), p. 32. (Hereinafter referred to as Bodley, *Clark*.)

2. Archibald Henderson, *The Conquest of the Old Southwest: The Romantic Story of the Early Pioneers into Virginia, the Carolinas, Tennessee, and Kentucky, 1740–1790* (New York: Century Co., 1920), p. 223–224. (Hereinafter referred to as Henderson, *Old Southwest.*) Skinner, *Pioneers,* pp. 132–134.

3. Robert Spencer Cotterill, "Richard Henderson," *Dictionary of American Biography,* 4: 531; Skinner, *Pioneers,* p. 140.

4. Quoted in Henderson, *Old Southwest,* pp. 237–238.

5. William C. Pendleton, *History of Tazewell County and Southwest Virginia, 1748–1920* (Richmond, Va.: W.C. Hill Printing Company, 1920), p. 259.

6. Julian P. Boyd, ed., *The Papers of Thomas Jefferson,* 20 vols. (Princeton, N.J.: Princeton University Press, 1950–1982), 1: 566. (Hereinafter referred to as Boyd, *Papers of Jefferson.*)

7. William L. Saunders, ed., *The Colonial Records of North Carolina, 1662–1776,* 10 vols. (Raleigh, N.C.: Josephus Daniels, Printer to the State, 1886–1890), 10: 385–386. John Bakeless, *Master of the Wilderness, Daniel Boone* (New York: William Morrow & Co., 1939), pp. 117–119. (Hereinafter referred to as Bakeless, *Boone.*)

8. *Fincastle County Virginia Court Record Book of Deeds,* May 20, 1774, February 8, 1775, Microfilm copy Virginia State Library, Richmond.

9. *Ibid.,* June 3, 1774.

10. Deposition of Arthur Campbell, before Samuel Hardy and Edward Charlton, in regard to purchase of lands by Richard Henderson & Co. from the Indians, Oct. 21, 1778. William P. Palmer, *et al.,* ed., *Calendar of Virginia State Papers and Other Manuscripts Preserved at the Capitol at Richmond,* 11 vols. (New York: Kraus Reprint Corp., 1968), 1: 303. (Hereinafter referred to as C.V.S.P.)

11. *Ibid.,* p. 304.

12. Deposition of Patrick Henry Esquire, June 4, 1777, *ibid.,* p. 289.

13. Henderson, *Old Southwest,* p. 240.

14. Boyd, *Papers of Jefferson,* 1 564.

15. *American Archives,* Series 4, 6, cols. 1528–1529.

16. *Ibid.,* col. 1533.

17. Henderson, *Old Southwest,* p. 257.

18. Robert McNutt McElroy, *Kentucky in the Nation's History* (New York:

Moffat, Yard and Company, 1909), pp. 57–60. (Hereinafter referred to as McElroy, *Kentucky*.) Selby, *Virginia*, p. 141.

19. *Journal of the House of Delegates of Virginia for 1776*. Microfilm copy, University of Georgia Library, Athens, Georgia, p. 11.

20. Bodley, *Clark*, p. 32; James Alton James, ed., *George Rogers Clark Papers, 1771–1781*, Vol. 3 of Virginia Series, *Collections of the Illinois State Historical Library*, 4 vols. (Springfield: Illinois State Historical Library, 1912), 214. For another perspective, see Selby, *Virginia*, pp. 141–144.

21. *Journal of the House, 1776*, pp. 19, 21, 34, 37; Bodley, *Clark*, p. 33.

22. Bodley, *Clark*, pp. 32–33.

23. *Ibid.*; *Journal of the House*, 1776, pp. 44, 90.

24. *Journal of the House*, 1776, pp. 44, 90.

25. Hening, *Statutes*, 9: 257–258.

26. Boyd, *Papers of Jefferson*, 1: 568–569.

27. Summers, *Southwest Virginia*, pp. 254–255; David Campbell to Lyman C. Draper, December 16, 1840, Draper Mss., 10DD7.

28. *Washington County Virginia Court Records, Minute Book I*, January 28, 1777, Microfilm copy, Virginia State Library, Richmond; Summers, *Southwest Virginia*, pp. 254–255.

29. *Washington Court, Minute Book I*, January 28, 1777.

30. Summers, *Southwest Virginia*, p. 262.

31. Hening, *Statutes*, 9: 26.

32. David Campbell to Lyman C. Draper, December 16, 1840, Draper Mss., 10DD7.

33. Summers, *Southwest Virginia*, p. 263.

34. *Ibid.*, pp. 263–264; *Journal of the House* (May–June 28, 1777), p. 28.

35. *Journal of the House* (May 5–June 28, 1777), pp. 67–68.

36. David Campbell to Lyman C. Draper, February 10, 1743, Draper Mss., 10DD36.

37. *Washington Court, Minute Book I*, p. 82.

38. Summers, *Southwest Virginia*, p. 300.

39. According to tradition, there was a contest among the citizens of the county as to the location of the county seat, some advocating Green

Springs as the proper site. Black's Fort won out because it was on the Great Road and because Thomas Walker, Joseph Black, and Samuel Briggs gave the county 120 acres of land for the purpose of locating a town and assisting in reducing the cost of erecting the necessary buildings. In addition, Walker agreed to sell another 484 acres of adjoining land to the trustees at a low price. The land was conveyed to the trustees October 7, 1781. See Summers, *Southwest Virginia*, p. 621.

40. *Journal of the House* (October 20, 1777–January 24, 1778), p. 17; Summers, *Southwest Virginia*, pp. 624–625.

41. Hening, *Statutes*, 9: 555; Summers, *Southwest Virginia*, p. 625.

42. Summers, *Southwest Virginia*, p. 67.

5. Revolution in the West

1. Commager and Morris, '*Seventy Six*, p. 505.

2. Alistair Cook, *America* (New York: Alfred A. Knopf, 1974), p. 110.

3. William L. Hall, Henry Reed McIlwaine, and George H. Reese, eds., *Journals of the Council of the State of Virginia*, 4 vols. (Richmond: Virginia State Library, 1931–1967), 1: 455. (Hereinafter referred to as *Journals of the Council*.) Summers, *Southwest Virginia*, pp. 261–262.

4. *Journals of the Council*, 2, 26–27.

5. Roosevelt, *Winning of the West*, 2, 227–228; Kincaid, "Arthur Campbell," p. 14; David Campbell to Lyman C. Draper, April 2, 1840, in Pilcher, *Historical Sketches*, p. 58.

6. Roosevelt, *Winning of the West*, 2, 231.

7. Summary of letter of Arthur Campbell to William Fleming, August 11, 1777, in Reuben Gold Thwaites and Louis Phelps Kellogg, eds., *Frontier Defense on the Upper Ohio, 1777–1778*, vol. 3, Draper Series (Madison: Wisconsin Historical Society, 1912): 38–39.

8. Kellogg, "Cornstalk"; *Dictionary of American Biography*, 4: 447–448.

9. Quoted in David I. Bushnell, Jr., "The Virginia Frontier in History—1778," *The Virginia Magazine of History and Biography*, 23 (April–October, 1914): 114–115. (Hereinafter referred to as Bushnell, "Virginia Frontier.")

10. Arthur Campbell to Charles Cummings, June 10, 1778, in Louis Phelps Kellogg, ed., *Frontier Advance on the Upper Ohio, 1778–1779*, vol. 4,

Draper Series (Madison: Wisconsin Historical Society, 1916): 85–87. (Hereinafter referred to as Kellogg, *Frontier Advance*.)

11. Daniel Smith to Arthur Campbell, June 19, 1778, Draper Mss., 9DD17.

12. Arthur Campbell to William Fleming, July 25, 1778, in Kellogg, *Frontier Advance*, p. 120.

13. Bushnell, "Virginia Frontier," p. 260; Harvey H. Jackson, *Lacklan McIntosh and the Politics of Revolutionary Georgia* (Athens: University of Georgia Press, 1979), p. 77.

14. Bushnell, "Virginia Frontier," p. 261; *Journals of the Council*, 2: 176–177.

15. Evan Shelby to Arthur Campbell, August 2, 1778, Draper Mss. 9DD1.

16. McElroy, *Kentucky*, pp. 85–96.

17. John D. Barnhart, *Henry Hamilton and George Rogers Clark in the American Revolution with the Unpublished Journal of Lieut. Gov. Henry Hamilton* (Crawfordsville, Indiana: R.E. Banta, 1951), pp. 79–85.

18. *Ibid.*, p. 200.

19. Albert V. Goodpasture, "Indian Wars and Warriors of the Old Southwest, 1730–1807," *Tennessee Historical Magazine*, 4 (March, 1918): 37–38.

20. David Campbell to Lyman C. Draper, June 1843, Draper Mss., 10DD43; Albert H. Tillson, Jr.'s, recent study of loyalism in the New River area emphasizes local conditions as a determining factor as to who was a Patriot or Loyalist. Tillson writes, "In the end, New River Valley loyalism's most prominent characteristic was its deep roots in the circumstance of life in local neighborhoods." According to Tillson, the Loyalists' primary enemies were local leaders like William Campbell, not national or state leaders. See "Localist Roots of Backcountry Loyalism," *The Journal of Southern History*, 54 (August, 1988): 403. (Hereinafter referred to as Tillson, "Loyalism.")

21. Bushnell, "Virginia Frontier," p. 115.

22. "The Preston Papers Relating to Western Virginia," *The Virginia Magazine of History and Biography*, 26 (October, 1918): 372n; Selby, *Virginia*, p. 219.

23. Quoted in Tillson, "Loyalism," p. 401.

24. Roosevelt, *Winning of the West*, II, 229.

25. Arthur Campbell to William Preston, July 3, 1780, in "The Preston Papers Relating to Western Virginia," *The Virginia Magazine of History and Biography*, 27 (April, 1919): 160–161.

26. Hening, *Statutes*, 10: 195.

27. Arthur Campbell to William Campbell, July 12, 1780, Draper Mss., 8DD3; Report of William Campbell, July or August, 1780, Draper Mss., 8DD4.

28. Henry B. Carrington, *Battles of the American Revolution 1775–1781, Including Battle Maps and Charts of the American Revolution* (n.p.: 1877; reprint ed., New York: Promontory Press, 1974) pp. 477–522. (Hereinafter referred to as Carrington, *Battles*.)

29. Memoirs of Arthur Campbell, in Lyman C. Draper, *Kings Mountain and Its Heroes: History of the Battle of Kings Mountain, October 7th, 1780, and the Events Which Led to It* (Baltimore, Md.: Genealogical Publishing Company, 1967), p. 527. (Hereinafter referred to as Draper, *Kings Mountain*.) Selby, *Virginia*, pp. 214–215.

30. *Ibid.*, p. 528.

31. *Ibid.*, p. 175.

32. An account by an unknown member of William Campbell's regiment, in *Ibid.*, pp. 529–530.

33. Summers, *Southwest Virginia*, pp. 853–855; State Committee on Compilation and Publication, *Roster of the Soldiers from North Carolina in the American Revolution* (Durham: North Carolina Daughters of the American Revolution, 1932; reprint, Baltimore: Genealogical Publishing Company, 1967), pp. 470–485.

34. Roosevelt, *Winning of the West*, 2: 256–257.

35. Summers, *Southwest Virginia*, pp. 326–327.

36. Campbell, "Memoirs," in Draper, *Kings Mountain*, pp. 525–526.

37. *Ibid.*, pp. 528–529.

38. Hugh Talmage Lefler and Albert Ray Newsome, *The History of a Southern State: North Carolina*, 3rd ed. (Chapel Hill: University of North Carolina Press, 1973), p. 250. (Hereinafter referred to as Lefler and Newsome, *North Carolina*.)

39. Henry Lumpkin, *From Savannah to Yorktown: The American Revolution in the South* (Columbia: University of South Carolina Press, 1981), p. 104. (Hereinafter referred to as Lumpkin, *Savannah to Yorktown*.)

40. Arthur Campbell to William Campbell, December 12, 1780, Campbell-Preston Papers, Microfilm copy, Library of Congress, Washington, D.C.

41. *Ibid.*; Arthur Campbell to Governor Jefferson, January 15, 1781; Draper Mss., 9DD24.

42. *Ibid.* Sevier was criticized for starting the campaign before Campbell and Martin arrived. It was complained at the time that Sevier was seeking glory for himself and also that his early movement apprised the Indians of the approach of the army before it was in a position to act efficiently. See Carl S. Driver, *John Sevier, Pioneer of the Old Southwest* (Chapel Hill: University of North Carolina Press, 1932), p. 25. (Hereinafter referred to as Driver, *Sevier*.)

43. Arthur Campbell to Governor Jefferson, January 15, 1781, *C.V.S.P.*, 1: 434–437; Colonel Campbell's Report of the Expedition Against the Cherokees, dated Washington County, January 15, 1781, Draper Mss., 9DD24. (Hereinafter referred to as "Campbell's Report.")

44. [Arthur Campbell's Message to the Cherokees], January 4, 1781, *C.V.S.P.* 1: 414–415.

45. David Campbell to Lyman C. Draper, December 16, 1840, Draper Mss., 10DD7; See appendix to no. 28, "Tennessee," in, *A Complete Historical Chronological and Geographical American Atlas* (Philadelphia: H.C. Carey and I. Lea, 1823).

46. Arthur Campbell to Governor Jefferson, January 15, 1781, *C.V.S.P.*, 1, 434–437; "Campbell's Report," January 15, 1781, Draper Mss., 9DD24. See also, Williams, *Tennessee*, pp. 181–191.

47. *Ibid.*

48. Thomas Jefferson to Arthur Campbell, February 17, 1781, in Boyd, *Papers of Jefferson*, 4: 634–635.

49. Williams, *Tennessee*, p. 191.

50. Boyd, *Papers of Jefferson*, 5:396n.

51. Arthur Campbell to Thomas Jefferson, March 28, 1781, in *ibid.*, p. 267–268.

52. Colonel Arthur Campbell to Governor Jefferson, April 25, 1781, *C.V.S.P.*, 2: 72–73.

53. William Christian to Thomas Jefferson, April 10, 1781, Boyd, *Papers of Jefferson*, 5: 395–396.

54. Arthur Campbell to George Rogers Clark, September 3, 1781, Draper Mss., 51J83.

55. Thomas Jefferson to the County Lieutenant of Washington and certain other counties, February 15, 1781, in Boyd, *Papers of Jefferson*, 5: 613–615.

56. Arthur Campbell to Thomas Jefferson, February 28, 1781, in *ibid.*, 5: 20.

57. Thomas Jefferson to the County Lieutenant of Washington County and certain other counties, May 28, 1781, in *ibid.*, 6: 24; Colonel Arthur Campbell to Governor Jefferson, June 14, 1781, *C.V.S.P.*, 2: 143.

58. Colonel William Preston to Governor Jefferson, April 13, 1781, *ibid.*, 2: 34–36.

59. James, *Clark Papers*, 8: 424.

60. Summary of letter of Arthur Campbell to William Preston, June 7, 1780, in Louis Phelps Kellogg, ed., *Frontier Retreat on the Upper Ohio, 1779–1781*, vol. 5, Draper Series (Madison: Wisconsin Historical Society, 1917): 192.

61. Quotes in Bodley, *Clark*, p. 163.

62. Arthur Campbell to William Edmiston, June 12, 1780, Draper Mss., 9DD20; Arthur Campbell to William Preston, June 13, 1780, Draper Ms., 5QQ33.

63. Bodley, *Clark*, p. 164.

64. John Floyd to Governor Jefferson, April 16, 1781, *C.V.S.P.*, 2: 47–49.

65. Quoted in Bodley, *Clark*, p. 199.

66. Quoted in *ibid.*, p. 203.

67. *Ibid.*, p. 208.

68. Colonel Arthur Campbell to Colonel William Davies, October 3, 1782, *C.V.S.P.*, 3: 337.

69. *Ibid.*

70. *Ibid.*

71. Lumpkin, *Savannah to Yorktown*, pp. 116–134, 163–175; Carrington, *Battles*, pp. 534–646.

72. Quoted in George Brown Tindall, *America: A Narrative History* (New York: W.W. Norton & Company, 1984), p. 226.

6. The Greater State of Franklin

1. Henry Steele Commager, ed., *Documents of American History*, 7th ed. (New York: Appleton-Century-Crofts, 1962), pp. 117–119.

2. Merrill Jensen, *The New Nation: A History of the United States During the Confederation, 1781–1789* (New York: Vintage Books, 1965), pp. 327–330. (Hereinafter referred to as Jensen, *New Nation.*)

3. Williams, *State of Franklin*, p. 6.

4. *Journals of the Continental Congress*, 18: 808.

5. *Ibid.*, 18: 915.

6. James W. Hagy and Stanley Folmsbee J., "Arthur Campbell and the Separate State Movements in Virginia and North Carolina," *The East Tennessee Historical Society's Publications*, (No. 42, 1970), p. 22. (Hereinafter referred to as Hagy and Folmsbee, "Separate State Movements.") Frederick Jackson Turner, "Western State-Making in the Revolutionary Era," *American Historical Review*, 1 (October-January, 1896); 74. (Hereinafter referred to as Turner, "State-Making.")

7. Hagy and Folmsbee, "Separate State Movements," p. 21.

8. John Sevier to Arthur Campbell, February 16, 1782, Arthur Campbell Papers.

9. William Christian to Arthur Campbell, February 19, 1782, Draper Mss., 9DD32; Williams, *State of Franklin*, p. 6.

10. *C.V.S.P.* 3: 414–415; Summers, *Southwest Virginia*, pp. 391–392; Williams, *State of Franklin*, p. 6.

11. See Appendix A; *C.V.S.P.* 4: 34–36.

12. *Ibid.*

13. Depositions of William Russell, March 10, 1786, and James Montgomery, March 14, 1786, *ibid.*, 4: 99, 103–104.

14. Arthur Campbell to Arthur Lee, June 9, 1782, in Williams, *State of Franklin*, p. 7; Hagy and Folmsbee, "Separate State Movements," p. 23.

15. Williams, *State of Franklin*, p. 26.

16. William Russell to Benjamin Harrison, September 25, 1783, *C.V.S.P.* 3: 532. See also, Summers, *Southwest Virginia*, p. 748; Pilcher, *Historical Sketches*, pp. 81–84; Lillian Stuart Butt, "The Political Career of Arthur Campbell" (unpublished M.A. thesis, University of Virginia, 1934), pp. 41–45.

17. *Journal of the House* (October 20–December 22, 1783), pp. 28, 41.

18. Commager, *Documents of American History*, pp. 121–123.

19. Walter Clark, ed., *The State Records of North Carolina* (Goldsboro: Nash

Brothers, Book and Job Printers, 1907) 24: 561–563. (Hereinafter referred to as *S.R.N.C.*) Haywood, *Civil and Political History of Tennessee*, pp. 494–497.

20. Ramsey, *Annals*, p. 287. George Henry Alden, "The State of Franklin." *American Historical Review*, 8 (January, 1903): 272–273. (Hereinafter referred to as Alden, "Franklin.")

21. Williams, *State of Franklin*, p. 39–41.

22. *Ibid.*, p. 44; Summers, *Southwest Virginia*, pp. 399–400.

23. David Campbell to Arthur Campbell, December 27, 1784, Arthur Campbell Papers.

24. *S.R.N.C.*, 24: 678–679.

25. Alden, "Franklin," p. 276–277; Stanley J. Folmsbee, Robert E. Corlew, and Enoch L. Mitchell, *Tennessee: A Short History* (Knoxville: University of Tennessee Press, 1969), p. 81. (Hereinafter referred to as Folmsbee, Corlew, Mitchell, *Tennessee*.) Hagy and Folmsbee, "Separate State Movements,"; p. 31.

26. Quoted in Williams, *State of Franklin*, p. 69.

27. Driver, *Sevier*, pp. 72–87.

28. Deposition of Andrew Kincanon, March 14, 1786, *C.V.S.P.*, 4: 105.

29. James Montgomery, William Edmiston, and Arthur Bowen to Patrick Henry, July 27, 1785, in William Wirt Henry, *Patrick Henry: Life, Correspondence and Speeches*, 3 vols. (New York: Charles Scribner's Sons, 1891), 3: 310–311.

30. Deposition of Thomas Berry, May 3, 1786, *C.V.S.P.*, 4: 127.

31. Ramsey, *Annals*, pp. 293–295; Driver, *Sevier*, p. 88; Summers, *Southwest Virginia*, p. 399.

32. Jensen, *New Nation*, p. 333; Thomas Perkins Abernethy, *From Frontier to Plantation in Tennessee: A Study in Frontier Democracy* (Tuscaloosa: University of Alabama Press, 1967), p. 76. (Hereinafter referred to as Abbernethy, *Frontier to Plantation*.) Williams, *State of Franklin*, 91. On October 7, 1782, Arthur Campbell was appointed a member of the board of trustees of Liberty Hall Academy, the forerunner of Washington and Lee University. See Hening, *Statutes*, 11: 164; William Henry Foote, *Sketches of Virginia, Historical and Biographical*, new ed. (Richmond, Va.: John Knox Press, 1966), p. 458.

33. Abernethy, *Frontier to Plantation*, p. 77.

34. *Ibid.*, p. 76; Williams, *State of Franklin*, pp. 90–94; Alden, "Franklin," pp. 274–275.

35. Abernethy, *Frontier to Plantation*, p. 77.

36. Jensen, *New Nation*, 333.

37. *Ibid.*

38. *Ibid.*

39. Alden, "Franklin," pp. 276–277.

40. See Appendix B; *S.R.N.C.*, 22: 637–640.

41. See Appendix C; *S.R.N.C.*, 22: 642–647.

42. Williams, *State of Franklin*, pp. 70–71.

43. Deposition of Arthur Bowen, March 10, 1786, *C.V.S.P.*, 4: 98.

44. Deposition of William Russell, March 10, 1786, *ibid.*, 99.

45. *Ibid.*, pp. 4–5; see Appendix D; National Archives Microfilm Publications, *Papers of the Continental Congress, 1774–1789: Memorials of the Inhabitants of Illinois, Kaskaski and Kentucky, 1780–1789.* Micro Copy no. 247, Roll 62, Item number 48 (Washington, D.C.: The National Archives and Records Service, 1959), pp. 283, 287. (Hereinafter referred to as *Papers of the Continental Congress.*) The *Papers of the Continental Congress* can also be found in Gaillard Hunt and Worthington C. Ford, eds., *Journals of the Continental Congress, 1774–1789*, 34 vols. (Washington, D.C.: National Archives, 1904–1937), 28: Item 48.

46. Turner, "State-Making," 259. Note Turner's map depicting new state projects in the West, 1772–1789, facing page 74. See also the map in Abernethy, *Western Lands*, p. 292.

47. J.T. McGill, "Franklin and Frankland: Names and Boundaries," *Tennessee Historical Magazine*, 8 (January, 1925): 248–257. McGill's article contains a map of the State of Franklin and Campbell's Greater State of Franklin.

48. See Appendix E; *Papers of the Continental Congress*; Micro Copy No. 247, Roll 62, Item 48, pp. 297–300.

49. Hening, *Statutes*, 11: 476–494; *Journals of the Council*, 3: 425–426.

50. *Journals of the Council*, 3: 451; Proclamation of Governor Henry, June 10, 1785, *C.V.S.P.*, 4: 34.

51. *C.V.S.P.*, 4: 42–43.

52. Deposition of William Russell, March 10, 1786, *ibid.*, p. 99.

53. Deposition of James Montgomery, March 14, 1786, *ibid.*, p. 103-104.

54. Summers, *Southwest Virginia*, pp. 404-405.

55. Arthur Campbell to Governor Henry, July 26, 1785, *C.V.S.P.*, 4: 44-45.

56. James Montgomery, William Edmiston and Arthur Bowen to Governor Henry, July 27, 1785, *ibid.*, pp. 45-46.

57. Henry's message to the General Assembly is in Ramsey, *Annals*, pp. 320-321.

58. Hening, *Statutes*, 12: 10.

59. *Ibid.*, pp. 41-42.

60. *Ibid.*, p. 37.

61. Samuel McDowell ot Arthur Campbell, September 23, 1787, Draper Mss., 9DD46; Harry Inns to Arthur Campbell, September 19, 1788, Draper Mss., 9DD51.

62. Arthur Campbell to Archibald Stuart, February 27, 1786, David Campbell Papers, Microfilm copy, Duke University, Durham, North Carolina.

63. Colonel Arthur Campbell to Governor Henry, June 3, 1785, *C.V.S.P.*, 4: 31.

64. Joseph Martin to Governor Patrick Henry, September 19, 1785, *ibid.*, pp. 53-54.

65. David Campbell to Lyman C. Draper, February 1, 1843 and February 16, 1843, Draper Mss., 10DD34, 10DD36; Lyman C. Draper to William Martin, February 18, 1843, Draper Mss., 3XX14.

66. William Edmiston, James Kincanon, Samuel Edmiston, James Thompson, and Arthur Bowen to the Executive, November 24, 1785, *C.V.S.P.*, 4: 69.

67. *Journals of the Council*, 3: 497.

68. *Ibid.*, pp. 497-498.

69. Russell's deposition is in *C.V.S.P.*, 4: 99. For other depositions see *C.V.S.P.*, 4: 93-144.

70. Deposition of Robert Craig, May 31, 1786, *ibid.*, pp. 140-142.

71. Arthur Campbell to His Excellency Patrick Henry, Esq'r. Governor of Virginia, and the honorable Council of State, April 3, 1786, *ibid.*, p. 113.

72. *Journals of the Council*, 3: 541–542.

73. *Ibid.*, p. 542.

74. William Edmiston, James Kincanon, Samuel Edmiston and James Thompson, Commissioners, to Governor Henry, June 2, 1786, in *C.V.S.P.*, 4: 143.

75. *Journals of the Council*, 3, 577.

76. Arthur Campbell and Robert Craig to Edmund Randolph, December 22, 1786, Arthur Campbell Papers.

77. Edmond Randolph to Arthur Campbell and others, December 23, 1786, Arthur Campbell Papers.

78. [Washington County Court to the Governor], Feb. 14, 1787, *C.V.S.P.*, 4: 237.

79. Edmiston v. Campbell, in *Virginia Reports, Jefferson-33 Grattan, 1730–1880*. Annotated under supervision of Thomas Johnson Michie, 26 vols. (Charlottesville, Va.: The Michie Company, Law Publishers, 1900–1904), 1:16. (Hereinafter referred to as *Virginia Reports*.)

80. "An action brought by an informer under a statute which establishes a penalty for the commission or omission of a certain act, and provides that the same shall be recoverable in a civil action, part of the penalty to go to any person who will bring such action and the remainder to the state...." See Henry Campbell Black, *Black's Law Dictionary* 4th ed. (St. Paul, Minn.: West Publishing Co., 1951), p. 144.

81. Edmiston v. Campbell, *Virginia Reports*, 1:16.

82. Williams, *State of Franklin*, pp. 184–225.

83. *Ibid.*, Folmsbee, Corlew, Mitchell, *Tennessee*, pp. 86–96.

84. Folmsbee, Corlew, Mitchell, *Tennessee*, p. 110.

85. Arthur Campbell to Arthur Lee, June 9, 1782, in Williams, *State of Franklin*, p. 7.

86. Arthur Campbell to Archibald Stuart, February 27, 1786, David Campbell Papers.

87. *Journal of the House* (October 15, 1787–January 8, 1788), p. 1; Summers, *Southwest Virginia*, p. 419.

7. Nationalist

1. Jensen, *New Nation*, p. 239.

2. Hugh Blair Grigsby, *The History of the Virginia Federal Convention of 1788* 2 vols. (Richmond: Virginia Historical Society, 1891), 1: 56–57; Hening, *Statutes*, 12: 462.

3. Jonathan Elliot, ed., *The Debates in the Several State Conventions on the Adoption of the Federal Constitution as Recommended by the General Convention at Philadelphia in 1787* 5 vols., 2nd ed. (Philadelphia: J.B. Lippincott Company, 1941), 3: 654–655; Grigsby, *Federal Convention*, 2: 345n.

4. Arthur Campbell to _____, August 15, 1794, Arthur Campbell Papers.

5. *Ibid.*

6. Arthur Campbell to Archibald Stuart, October 31, 1785, David Campbell Papers.

7. Arthur Campbell to _____, August 15, 1794, Arthur Campbell Papers.

8. Arthur Campbell to Archibald Stuart, probably late July or early August, 1789, Draper Mss., 9DD56.

9. *Ibid.*, Arthur Campbell to Arthur Lee, June 9, 1782, in Williams, *State of Franklin*, pp. 7–8.

10. Samuel McDowell to Arthur Campbell, June 22, 1790, Draper Mss., 9DD.

11. Arthur Campbell to _____, August 15, 1794, Arthur Campbell Papers.

12. Arthur Campbell to George Washington, May 10, 1789, Arthur Campbell Papers.

13. George Washington to Arthur Campbell, September 15, 1789, Fitzpatrick, *Writings of Washington*, 30: 403–404.

14. Secretary of War Henry Knox to Arthur Campbell, September 15, 1789, Fitzpatrick, *Writings of Washington*, 30: 403–404.

14. Secretary of War Henry Knox to Arthur Campbell, December 10, 1789, Draper Mss., 9DD55.

15. Charles J. Kappler, ed., *Indian Affairs; Laws and Treaties* 2 vols. (Washington, D.C.: U.S. Government Printing Office, 1903), 2: 6–8. (Hereinafter referred to as Kappler, *Indian Treaties*.) George Dewey

Harmon, *Sixty Years of Indian Affairs, Political, Economic, and Diplomatic, 1789-1850* (Chapel Hill: University of North Carolina Press, 1941), pp. 42–43. (Hereinafter referred to as Harmon, *Sixty Years of Indian Affairs.)*

16. Goodpasture, "Indian Wars," pp. 128–145.

17. Kappler, *Indian Treaties*, 2: 22–25; Harmon, *Sixty Years of Indian Affairs*, p. 45.

18. Colonel Arthur Campbell to Governor Randolph, December 31, 1787, C.V.S.P., 4: 375.

19. Arthur Campbell to John Brown, December 29, 1787, Arthur Campbell Papers.

20. Colonel Arthur Campbell to Governor Beverly Randolph, July 20, 1789, C.V.S.P., 5: 4–5.

21. [Arthur Campbell's Talk to the Cherokees], March 3, 1787, *ibid.,* 4: 249–250.

22. John Watts was the son of a white man who resided with the Cherokees. His mother was the sister of Tassel. Watts, like Dragging Canoe, had refused to take part in the Treaty of Long Island in 1777 and left the Overhill towns rather than submit to the authority of the United States. See Goodpasture, "Indian War," p. 172.

23. *Ibid.,* pp. 185–195; Brown, *Old Frontiers*, pp. 358–361.

24. Arthur Campbell to the Governor, November 1, 1792, C.V.S.P., 4: 121–122.

25. Brown, *Old Frontiers*, p. 366.

26. Summers, *Southwest Virginia*, pp. 696–703.

27. Arthur Campbell to William Blount, June, 1792, Draper Mss., 9DD69.

28. *Ibid.*

29. David [William] Blount to the Governor, September 2, 1792, C.V.S.P., 6: 52–53.

30. Arthur Campbell to Governor Henry Lee, October 17, 1792, *ibid.,* 6: 100–101.

31. Summers, *Southwest Virginia*, pp. 704–746.

32. Andrew Lewis to the Governor, August 17, 1793, C.V.S.P., 6: 484–485.

33. Andrew Lewis to the Governor, September 12, 1793, *ibid.,* pp. 527–528.

34. Arthur Campbell's Remarks on Captain A. Lewis' letter dated September 12th, 1793, *ibid.*, pp. 528–530.

35. Arthur Campbell to the Governor, October 11, 1793, *ibid.*, pp. 627–629.

36. A. Lewis to Col. Arthur Campbell; and Arthur Campbell's Reply, Endorsed on Same Paper, November 7, 1793, *ibid.*, pp. 627–629.

37. Arthur Bowers Certificate as to Colonel Arthur Campbell, September 7, 1793, *ibid.*, pp. 519.

38. Affidavits as to Colonel Arthur Campbell, October 14, 1793, *ibid.*, pp. 597.

39. Mathew Willoughby's Memorial to the Executive, August 27, 1793, *ibid.*, pp. 497–498.

40. Certificate of David Young, October 26, 1793, *ibid.*, pp. 133–135.

41. Arthur Campbell to the Governor, May 8, 1794, *ibid.*, pp. 133–135.

42. Summers, *Southwest Virginia*, p. 435.

43. *Ibid.*, p. 436.

44. An account of the captivity of Mrs. Elizabeth Levingston, April 15, 1794, C.V.S.P., 7:3.

45. Arthur Campbell, Commanding Western Militia, to the Governor, April 21, and 29, 1794, *ibid.*, pp. 117–118, 123–124.

46. Summers, *Southwest Virginia*, p. 443.

47. *Ibid.*

48. Harmon, *Sixty Years of Indian Affairs*, p. 47.

49. *Ibid.*, p. 437.

50. Postmaster General to Arthur Campbell, September 8, 1794, Carter, *Territorial Papers*, 4: 354.

51. Postmaster General to Arthur Campbell, December 22, 1794, *ibid.*, p. 376.

52. Postmaster General to Arthur Campbell, January 15, 1796, *ibid.*, pp. 416–417.

53. Postmaster General to Arthur Campbell, August 15, 1796, *ibid.*, p. 417n.

54. Postmaster General to Arthur Campbell, November 4, 1796, *ibid.*

55. Arthur Campbell to Senator Joseph Anderson, February 13, 1798, Pickering Papers, 22: 42.

56. Arthur Campbell to Timothy Pickering, June 8, 1779, *ibid.*, 24: 301.

57. Arthur Campbell to Timothy Pickering, October 16, 1798, *ibid.*, 23: 233; January 12, 1799, 24: 17.

58. Arthur Campbell to Timothy Pickering, August 15, 1799, *ibid.*, 25: 101.

59. At the death of Washington, December 14, 1799, Campbell wrote a eulogy, 16 pages long, to be read before the faculty and students of Washington College. See Arthur Campbell to Timothy Pickering, February 21, 1800, *ibid.*, 26: 30.

60. Arthur Campbell to George Washington, February 18, 1796, Carter, *Territorial Papers*, 4: 420. Campbell was motivated by his opposition to the Sevier and Blount speculative interests. While Campbell recognized the authority of the Federal Government over Indian lands, he was sympathetic toward the settlers in Tennessee who were living beyond the boundary lines established by treaties between the Government and Cherokee Nation. He did not favor defiance of the government but thought justice required that congress favorably consider petitions of settlers who were being removed by federal troops from lands they had settled on. His views were fully elaborated in the *Knoxville Gazette* in April, 1797, under the signature of "Campbell." Although it is by no means certain that Arthur Campbell wrote the appeals that appeared in the *Gazette*, it was generally assumed that he did, and they do express his thinking on the subject. See *Roulstone's Knoxville Gazette and Weekly Advertiser*, Monday, April 3, 1797, p. 4, Microfilm copy, Tennessee State Library, Nashville; Ramsey, *Annals*, pp. 681–686.

61. William H. Masterson, *William Blount* (Baton Rouge: Louisiana State University Press, 1954), pp. 304–342.

62. Arthur Campbell to Timothy Pickering, July 29, 1797, Pickering Papers, 21: 192.

63. Arthur Campbell to Timothy Pickering, August 7, 1797, *ibid.*, 21: 208.

64. *Ibid.*

65. Timothy Pickering to Arthur Campbell, August 18, 1797, *ibid.*, 7: 93.

66. Arthur Campbell to Timothy Pickering, October 1, 1797, *ibid.*, 21: 227.

67. Arthur Campbell to David Campbell, July 11, 1798, David Campbell Papers.

68. Thomas Jefferson to Colonel Arthur Campbell, September 1, 1797, in

Paul Leicester Ford, ed., *The Works of Thomas Jefferson*, 12 vols. (New York: G.P. Putnam's Sons, 1904–1905), 8: 336–338. (Hereinafter referred to as Ford, *Jefferson.*)

69. Arthur Campbell to Timothy Pickering, November 23, 1798, Pickering Papers, 23: 328.

70. Thomas Jefferson to Colonel Arthur Campbell, September 1, 1797, Ford, *Jefferson,* 8: 336–338.

71. Arthur Campbell to Timothy Pickering, July 2, 1799, Pickering Papers, 25: 8. This letter was sent to Campbell's nephew, David Campbell. See Arthur Campbell to David Campbell, January 29, 1799, David Campbell Papers.

72. Arthur Campbell to Timothy Pickering, October 7, 1797, *ibid.,* 21: 292; November 23, 1798, 33: 328; September 14, 1799, 25: 155.

73. Summers, *Southwest Virginia,* p. 446.

8. The Final Years

1. U.S. Office of the Census, *Second Census, 1800 Return of the Whole Number of Persons Within the Several Districts of the United States* (Washington, D.C.: Duane, Printer, 1801), p. 21.

2. George Madison, Auditor's Office Receipt to Arthur Campbell, October 20, 1796, Kentucky Land Papers in the Arthur Campbell Papers. See also the Tennessee and North Carolina Land Papers, and the Virginia Land Papers in the Arthur Campbell Papers.

3. See the genealogy section in the Arthur Campbell Papers. See also Washington Court, *Minute Book I,* p. 6.

4. The author found no record of Campbell's ever having owned slaves, although a few blacks may have worked for him. His will indicates that he had no slaves in 1811 but he provided for the purchase of slaves to attend his wife and daughters after his death. See the "Last Will and Testament" of Arthur Campbell, *Will Book Number A,* pp. 38–45, on file at the Courthouse, Knox County, Kentucky.

5. Kincaid, "Arthur Campbell," p. 16.

6. Arthur Campbell to Charles Cummings, December 25, 1802, Draper Mss., 9DD16.

7. His correspondence in the David Campbell Papers shows where

Campbell was during these years and supports the view that he settled in Kentucky around 1809.

8. Arthur Campbell to David Campbell, June 11, 1804, David Campbell Papers.

9. Arthur Campbell to Miss Peggy Campbell, June 11, 1801, Sayers, *Pathfinders*, pp. 229–230.

10. Arthur Campbell to Miss Peggy Campbell, May 14, 1803, in *ibid.*, p. 230.

11. These valuable personal letters are in *ibid.*, pp. 230–233.

12. Arthur Campbell to John Campbell, October 30, 1809, David Campbell Papers.

13. Arthur Campbell to David Campbell, March 13, 1810, *ibid.*

14. Arthur Campbell to David Campbell, August 18, 1810, *ibid.*

15. Arthur Campbell to David Campbell, July 6, July 17, August 18, 1810, *ibid.*

16. Arthur Campbell to Charles Cummings, December 25, 1802, Draper Mss., 9DD76.

17. Arthur Campbell to David Campbell, August 22, 1803 and February 7, 1811, David Campbell Papers.

18. Arthur Campbell to Miss Peggy Campbell, May 12, 1808, Sayers, *Pathfinders*, p. 232.

19. Arthur Lee Campbell to David Campbell, August 25, 1811, 9DD83.

20. Campbell, "Will" Kincaid, "Arthur Campbell," p. 18.

21. Campbell, "Will."

22. Henderson, *Old Southwest*, ix–x.

23. Quoted in Summers, *Southwest Virginia*, pp. 463–464, and Kincaid, "Arthur Campbell," p. 2–3. According to Kincaid, the broken tombstone was discovered in May, 1890, when workmen were digging up 24th Street in Middlesboro, Kentucky. The Daughters of the American Revolution erected a marker to the memory of Campbell on Cumberland Avenue, some distance from the grave site. A house now stands on the original burial place.

Bibliography

Primary Sources

Manuscripts

Duke University, Durham. David Campbell Papers. Microfilm copy.

Filson Club, Louisville, Kentucky. Arthur Campbell Papers. Microfilm copy.

"Last Will and Testament of Arthur Campbell." *Will Book Number A.* On file at the County Courthouse, Knox County, Kentucky.

Library of Congress, Washington, D.C. Campbell-Preston Papers. Microfilm copy.

Massachusetts Historical Society Collections, Boston. Timothy Pickering Papers. Microfilm copy, University of Georgia Library, Athens, Georgia.

National Archives, Washington, D.C. *Papers of the Continental Congress, 1774–1789: Memorials of the Inhabitants of Illinois, Kaskaski and Kentucky 1780–1789.* Micro Copy no 247, Roll 62, Item number 48. Microfilm copy, University of Georgia Library, Athens, Georgia.

Virginia State Library, Richmond. *Botetourt County Court Records, Order Book I, 1770–1771.* Microfilm copy.

_____. *Fincastle County Virginia Court Records, Order Book I, 1773–1788.* Microfilm copy.

_____. *Fincastle County Virginia Record Book of Deeds.* Microfilm copy.

_____. *Washington County Virginia Court Records, Minute Book I.* Microfilm copy.

Wisconsin State Historical Society, Madison. Lyman C. Draper Collection. Microfilm copy, University of Georgia, Athens, Georgia.

Published

Boyd, Julian P., ed. *The Papers of Thomas Jefferson.* 20 vols. Princeton, N.J.: Princeton University Press, 1950–1982.

Carter, Clarence Edwin, ed. *The Territorial Papers of the United States.* Vol. 4: *The Territory South of the River Ohio, 1790–1796.* Washington, D.C.: United States Government Printing Office, 1936.

Chalkley, Lyman, ed. *Chronicles of the Scotch-Irish Settlements in Virginia.* Reprint. 3 vols. Baltimore, Md.: Genealogical Publishing Co., 1965.

Clark, Walter, ed. *The State Records of North Carolina,* 16 vols. Goldsboro: N.C.: Nash Brothers, Book and Job Printers, 1895–1907. *The State Records of North Carolina* begin with vol. 11, a continuation of William L. Saunders, ed., *Colonial Records of North Carolina,* 10 vols.

Commanger, Henry Steele, and Morris, Richard B., eds. *The Spirit of 'Seventy-Six: The Story of the American Revolution as Told by Participants.* New York: Harper & Row, Publishers, 1967.

Elliot, Jonathan, ed. *The Debates in the Several State Conventions on the Adoption of the Federal Constitution as Recommended by the General Convention at Philadelphia in 1787.* 2nd ed. 5 vols. Philadelphia; J.B. Lippincott Company, 1941.

Fitzpatrick, John C., ed. *The Diaries of George Washington, 1748–1799.* 4 vols. Boston: Houghton Mifflin Company, 1925.

_____. *The Writings of George Washington from the Original Manuscript Sources, 1745–1799.* 39 vols. Washington, D.C.: United States Government Printing Office, 1931–1944.

Force, Peter, ed. *American Archives: A Documentary History of the English Colonies in North America,* 4th Series, 6 vols. Washington, D.C.: M. St. Clair Clark and Peter Force, 1846.

Ford, Paul Leicester, ed. *The Works of Thomas Jefferson.* 12 vols. New York: G.P. Putnam's Sons, 1904–1905.

Ford, Worthington Chauncey, ed. *Journals of the Continental Congress, 1774–1789.* 34 vols. Washington, D.C.: U.S. Government Printing Office, 1906.

Hall, William L., McIlwaine, Henry Reed, and Reese, George H., eds. *Journals of the Council of State of Virginia*. 4 vols. Richmond: Virginia State Library, 1931–1967.

Harwell, Richard Barksdale, ed. *The Committees of Westmoreland and Fincastle: Proceedings of the County Committees, 1774–1776*. Richmond: Virginia State Library, 1956.

Hening, William Waller, ed. *The Statutes at Large; Being a Collection of all the Laws of Virginia from the First Session of the Legislature, in the Year 1619*. 13 vols. Richmond, Va.: Franklin Press, 1809–1823.

Hunt, Gaillard, and Ford, Warthington C., eds. *Journals of the Continental Congress, 1774–1789*. 34 vols. Washington, D.C.: National Archives, 1904–1937.

James, James Alton, ed., *George Rogers Clark Papers, 1771–1781*. Vol. III of Virginia Series, *Collections of the Illinois State Historical Library*. 4 vols. Springfield: Illinois State Historical Library, 1912.

Journals of the House of Delegates of Virginia. Microfilm copy, University of Georgia Library, Athens, Georgia.

Kappler, Charles J., ed. *Indian Affairs: Laws and Treaties*. 2 vols. Washington, D.C.: U.S. Government Printing Office, 1903.

Kellogg, Louise Phelps, ed. *Frontier Advance on the Upper Ohio, 1787–1779*. Vol. 4 of Draper Series, *Publications of the State Historical Society of Wisconsin*. 5 vols. Madison: State Historical Society of Wisconsin, 1916.

_____. *Frontier Retreat on the Upper Ohio, 1779–1781*. Vol. 5 of Draper Series, *Publications of the State Historical Society of Wisconsin*. 5 vols. Madison: State Historical Society of Wisconsin, 1917.

_____. *Frontier Defense on the Upper Ohio, 1777–1778*. Vol. 3 of Draper Series, *Publications of the State Historical Society of Wisconsin*. 5 vols. Madison: State Historical Society of Wisconsin, 1912.

_____, and Twaites, Ruben Gold, eds. *Documentary History of Dunmore's War, 1774*. Madison: Wisconsin Historical Society, 1905.

Kennedy, John Pendleton, ed. *Journals of the House of Burgesses of Virginia*. 13 vols. Richmond, Va.: The Colonial Press, E. Waddey Co., 1905–1915.

Palmer, William P., et al., ed. *Calendar of Virginia State Papers and Other Manuscripts Preserved at the Capitol at Richmond*. Reprint. 11 vols. New York: Kraus Reprint Corp., 1968.

"The Preston Papers Relating to Western Virginia." *The Virginia Magazine of History and Biography*, 26 (October, 1918): 363–379.

Roulstone's Knoxville Gazette and Weekly Advertiser, April, 1797. Microfilm copy, Tennessee State Library, Nashville.

Saunders, William L., ed. *The Colonial Records of North Carolina, 1662–1776.* 10 vols. Raleigh, N.C.: Josephus Daniels, Printer to the State, 1886–1890.

Smith, James. *An Account of the Remarkable Occurrences in the Life and Travels of Col. James Smith.* Lexington, Ky.: John Bradford, 1799. Microcard copy, University of Georgia Library, Athens, Georgia.

Tarter, Brent, Schrubner, Robert L.; and Van Schreeven, William J., eds., *Revolutionary Virginia: The Road to Independence.* 7 vols. Charlottsville: University Press of Virginia, 1973–1983.

U.S. Office of the Census. *Second Census, 1800, Return of the Whole Number of Persons Within the Several Districts of the United States.* Washington, D.C.: Duane, Printer, 1801.

Secondary Sources

Books

Abernethy, Thomas Perkins. *From Frontier to Plantation in Tennessee: A Study in Frontier Democracy.* Tuscaloosa: University of Alabama Press, 1967.

_____. *Western Lands and the American Revolution.* New York: D. Appleton-Century Company, 1937.

Barck Jr., Oscar T., and Lefler, Hugh T. *Colonial American.* London: Collier-Macmillan, 1969.

Barnhart, John D. *Henry Hamilton and George Rogers Clark in the American Revolution, with the Unpublished Journal of Lieut. Gov. Henry Hamilton.* Crawfordville, Indiana: R.E. Banta, 1951.

Becker, Carl Lotus, *Beginnings of the American People.* Boston: Houghton Mifflin, 1915; reprint ed., Ithaca, N.Y.: Cornell University Press, 1966.

Billings, Warren M.; Selby, John E., and Tate, Thad W. *Colonial Virginia: A History.* White Plains, N.Y.: KTO Press, 1986.

Black, Henry Campbell. *Black's Law Dictionary.* 4th ed. St. Paul, Minn.: West Publishing Co., 1951.

Bodley, Temple. *George Rogers Clark: His Life and Public Services*. Boston: Houghton Mifflin Company, 1926.

Brown, John P. *Old Frontiers: The Story of the Cherokee Indians from Earliest Times to the Date of Their Removal to the West, 1838*. Kingsport, Tenn.: Southern Publishers, Inc., 1938.

Burnett, Edmund Cody. *The Continental Congress*. New York: W.W. Norton & Company, 1964.

Campbell, Leslie Lyle. *The Campbell Clan in Virginia*. Lexington, Va.: n.p., 1954.

Carrington, Henry B. *Battles of the American Revolution, 1775–1781, Including Battle Maps and Charts of the American Revolution*. N.p.: 1877; reprint ed., New York: Promontory Press, 1974.

A Complete Historical Chronological and Geographical American Atlas. Philadelphia: H.C. Carey and I. Lea, 1823.

Cook, Alistair. *America*. New York: Alfred A. Knopf, 1974.

Cotterill, Robert Spencer. "Richard Henderson" in *Dictionary of American Biography*. 17 vols. Edited by Allen Johnson, et al. New York: Charles Scribner's Sons, 1964–1981. 4: 530–531.

_____. *The Southern Indians: The Story of the Civilized Tribes Before Removal*. Norman: University of Oklahoma Press, 1954.

Crane, Katherine Elizabeth. "Oconostota." *Dictionary of American Biography*. 7: 621–622.

Draper, Lyman C. *Kings Mountain and Its Heroes: History of the Battle of Kings Mountain, October 7th, 1780, and the Events Which Led to It*. Baltimore, Md.: Genealogical Publishing Company, 1967.

Driver, Carl, S. *John Sevier, Pioneer of the Old Southwest*. Chapel Hill: University of North Carolina Press, 1932.

Eckenrode, H.J. *The Revolution in Virginia*. Boston: Houghton Mifflin Company, 1916.

Folmsbee, Stanley J.; Corlew, Robert E.; and Mitchell, Enoch L. *Tennessee: A Short History*. Knoxville: University of Tennessee Press, 1969.

Foote, William Henry. *Sketches of Virginia; Historical and Biographical*. New ed. Richmond, Va.: John Knox Press, 1866.

Ford, Henry Jones. *The Scotch-Irish in America*. Princeton, N.J.: Princeton University Press, 1915.

Gipson, Lawrence Henry. *The Coming of the Revolution, 1763–1775*. New York: Harper & Row, Publishers, 1954.

Grigsby, Hugh Blair. *The History of the Virginia Federal Convention of 1788.* 2 vols. Richmond: Virginia Historical Society, 1891.

————. *The Virginia Convention of 1776.* Richmond, Va.: J.W. Randolph, 1855.

Hansen, Marcus Lee. *The Atlantic Migration, 1607–1860: A History of the Continuing Settlement of the United States.* New York: Harper & Row, Publishers, 1961.

Harmon, George Dewey. *Sixty Years of Indian Affairs, Political, Economic, and Diplomatic, 1789–1850.* Chapel Hill: University of North Carolina Press, 1941.

Hawke, David. *The Colonial Experience.* New York: Bobbs Merrill Company, 1966.

Haywood, John. *The Civil and Political History of the State of Tennessee from Its Earliest Settlement Up to the Year 1796, Including Boundaries of the State.* Nashville, Tenn.: Publishing House of the Methodist Episcopal Church, South, 1891.

Henderson, Archibald. *The Conquest of the Old Southwest: The Romantic Story of the Early Pioneers Into Virginia, the Carolinas, Tennessee, and Kentucky, 1740–1790.* New York: Century Co., 1920.

Henry, William Wirt. *Patrick Henry: Life, Correspondence and Speeches.* 3 vols. New York: Charles Scribner's Sons, 1891.

Hodge, Frederick Webb, ed. *Handbook of the American Indians.* Part 1, Bulletin no. 30, *Bureau of American Ethnology.* Washington, D.C.: U.S. Government Printing Office, 1907.

Howe, Henry. *Historical Collections of Virginia.* Charleston, S.C.: Babcock & Company, 1845.

Jackson, Harvey H. *Lachlan McIntosh and the Politics of Revolutionary Georgia.* Athens: University of Georgia Press, 1979.

Jensen, Merrill. *The New Nation: A History of the United States During the Confederation, 1781–1789.* New York: Vintage Books, 1965.

Kellogg, Louis Phelps, "Cornstalk." *Dictionary of American Biography.* 2: 447–448.

Kincaid, Robert L. *The Wilderness Road.* New York: Bobbs Merrill Company, 1947.

Lefler, Hugh Talmage, and Newsome, Albert Ray. *The History of a Southern State: North Carolina.* 3rd ed. Chapel Hill: University of North Carolina Press, 1973.

Lewis, Virgil Anson. *History of the Battle of the Point Pleasant, Fought Between White Men and Indians at the Mouth of the Great Kanawha River (New Point Pleasant, West Virginia) Monday, October, 10th, 1774. The Chief Event of Dunmore's War.* Charleston, W. Va.: The Tribune Printing Company, 1909.

Lumpkin, Henry. *From Savannah to Yorktown: The American Revolution in the South.* Columbia: University of South Carolina Press, 1981.

McElroy, Robert McNutt. *Kentucky in the Nation's History.* New York: Moffat, Yard and Company, 1909.

Masterson, William H. *William Blount.* Baton Rouge: Louisiana State University Press, 1954.

Miller, John C. *Origins of the American Revolution.* Stanford, Calif.: Stanford University Press, 1959.

Parkman, Francis. *The Conspiracy of Pontiac and the Indian War After the conquest of Canada.* 2 vols. Boston: Little, Brown, and Company, 1902.

Pendleton, William C. *History of Tazewell County and Southwest Virginia, 1748–1920.* Richmond, Va.: W.C. Hill Printing Company, 1920.

Peyton, John Lewis. *History of Augusta County, Virginia.* 2nd ed. Bridgewater, Va.: n.p., 1953.

Pilcher, Margaret Campbell. *Historical Sketches of the Campbell, Pilcher and Kindred Families, Including the Bowen, Russell, Owen, Grant, Goodwin, Amis, Carothers, Hope, Faliaferro, and Powell Families.* Nashville, Tenn.: Press of Marshall & Bruce Co., 1911.

Ramsey, J.G.M. *The Annals of Tennessee to the End of the Eighteenth Century.* Reprint, Knoxville, Tenn.: n.p., 1967.

Roosevelt, Theodore. *The Winning of the West.* 4 vols. New York: G.P. Putnam's Sons, 1895–1898.

Sayers, Elizabeth Lemmon. *Pathfinders and Patriots.* Marion, Va.: Smyth County Historical and Museum Society, Inc., 1983.

Selby, John E. *The Revolution in Virginia, 1775–1783.* Williamsburg, Va.: Colonial Williamsburg Foundation, 1988.

Skinner, Constance L. *Pioneers of the Old Southwest.* New York: United States Publishers Association, Inc., 1919.

Sosin, Jack M. *The Revolutionary Frontier, 1763–1793.* New York: Holt, Rinehart and Winston, 1967.

State Committee on Compilation and Publication. *Roster of the Soldiers from North Carolina in the American Revolution.* Durham: North Carolina Daughters of the American Revolution, 1932; reprint, Baltimore: Genealogical Publishing Company, 1967.

Summers, Lewis Preston. *History of Southwest Virginia, 1746–1786, Washington County, 1777–1870.* Richmond, Va.: J.L. Hill Printing Company, 1903.

Tindall, George Brown. *America: A Narrative History.* New York: W.W. Norton & Company, 1984.

Van Tyne, Claude H. *The Causes of the War of Independence.* New York: Peter Smith, 1952.

Virginia Reports, Jefferson — 33 Gratan, 1730–1880. Annotated under supervision of Thomas Johnson Michie. 26 vols. Charlottesville, Va.: Michie Company, Law Publishers, 1900–1904.

Waddell, Joseph A. *Annals of Augusta County, Virginia.* Richmond, Va.: Wm. Ellis Jones, Book and Job Printer, 1886.

Williams, Samuel Cole. *History of the Lost State of Franklin.* Johnson City, Tenn.: Watauga Press, 1924.

————. *Tennessee During the Revolutionary War.* Nashville: Tennessee Historical Commission, 1944.

Wilson, Goodridge. *Smyth County History and Traditions.* Radford, Va.: Commonwealth Press, Inc., 1932.

Wilson, Howard McKnight. *Great Valley Patriots: Western Virginia in the Struggle for Liberty.* Verona, Va.: McClure Printing Company, Inc., 1976.

Wilson, Thomas C., Jr., ed. *Washington and Lee University Alumni Directory, 1749–1940.* Lexington, Va.: McClure Printing Company, Inc., 1976.

Withers, Alexander Scott. *Chronicles of Border Warfare or a History of the Settlement by the Whites of Northwestern Virginia and the Indian Wars and Massacres.* Clarksburg, Va.: Published by Joseph Israel, 1831. Microcard copy, University of Georgia Library, Athens, Georgia.

Wroth, Lawrence C. "James Logan." *Dictionary of American Biography.* 6: 362–363.

Articles and Bulletins

Alden, George Henry. "The State of Franklin." *American Historical Review* 8 (January 1903): 271–289.

Bushnell, David I., Jr. "The Virginia Frontier in History, 1778." *The Virginia Magazine of History and Biography* 23 (April–October, 1915): 113–123; 256–258; 336–351.

Chitwood, Oliver Perry. "Justice in Colonial Virginia." *Johns Hopkins University Studies in Historical and Political Science* 23 (July–August, 1905): 472–492.

Coleman, Charles Washington. "The County Committees of 1774–75 in Virginia." *William and Mary College Quarterly Historical Magazine*, series 1, 5 (October 1898): 94–106.

Ganyard, Robert L. "Threat from the West: North Carolina and the Cherokee, 1776–1778." *The North Carolina Historical Review* 45 (Winter, 1968): 47–66.

Goodpasture, Albert V. "Indian Wars and Warriors of the Old Southwest, 1730–1807." *Tennessee Historical Magazine* 4 (March–September): 3–49; 106–145; 156–157; 161–210.

Hagy, James W., and Folmsbee, Stanley J. "Arthur Campbell and the Separate State Movements in Virginia and North Carolina." *The East Tennessee Historical Society's Publications* 42 (1970), 20–46.

Ingle, Edward. "Justices of the Peace of Colonial Virginia, 1757–1775." *Bulletin of the Virginia State Library* 14 (April–July, 1921).

Kemper, Charles E. "The Settlement of the Valley." *Virginia Magazine of History and Biography* 30 (January, 1922): 169–182.

Kincaid, Robert L. "Colonel Arthur Campbell: Frontier Leader and Patriot." *The Historical Society of Washington County, Virginia, Publications*, series 2, no. 1 (Fall, 1965).

Koontz, Louis K. "The Virginia Frontier, 1754–1763." *Johns Hopkins Studies in Historical and Political Science* 43 (No. 2, 1925), 185–370.

McGill, J.T. "Franklin and Frankland: Names and Boundaries." *Tennessee Historical Magazine* 8 (January, 1925): 248–257.

Tillson, Albert H. "The Localist Roots of Backcountry Loyalism: An Examination of Popular Political Culture in Virginia's New River Valley." *The Journal of Southern History* 44 (August, 1988): 387–404.

Turner, Frederick Jackson. "Western State-Making in the Revolutionary Era." *American Historical Review* 2 (October–January, 1896): 70–87, 251–269.

Williams, Samuel Cole. "Shelby's Fort." *The East Tennessee Historical Society's Publications* 7 (1935): 28–37.

Unpublished Material

Butt, Lillian Stuart. "The Political Career of Arthur Campbell." M.A. Thesis, University of Virginia, 1934.

Index